AWAKENING TO THE INFINITE

Awakening
to the Infinite

Essential Answers for Spiritual Seekers
from the Perspective of Nonduality

SWAMI MUKTANANDA OF RISHIKESH

North Atlantic Books
Berkeley, California

First published in French as *L'Éveil à l'Infini: réponses essentielles à tout chercheur spirituel* by Éditions A.L.T.E.S.S.
Copyright © 2013 by Éditions A.L.T.E.S.S.

Published by
North Atlantic Books
P.O. Box 12327
Berkeley, California 94712

Cover photo of Swami Muktananda of Rishikesh by Yves Devaddère
Cover photo by Philip Yuan/Shutterstock.com
Cover and book design by Claudia Smelser
Printed in the United States of America

Awakening to the Infinite: Essential Answers for Spiritual Seekers from the Perspective of Nonduality is sponsored and published by the Society for the Study of Native Arts and Sciences (dba North Atlantic Books), an educational nonprofit based in Berkeley, California, that collaborates with partners to develop cross-cultural perspectives, nurture holistic views of art, science, the humanities, and healing, and seed personal and global transformation by publishing work on the relationship of body, spirit, and nature.

North Atlantic Books' publications are available through most bookstores. For further information, visit our website at www.northatlanticbooks.com or call 800-733-3000.

LIBRARY OF CONGRESS CATALOGING-IN-PUBLICATION DATA
Muktananda, Swami.
  Awakening to the infinite : essential answers for spiritual seekers from the perspective of nonduality / Swami Muktananda of Rishikesh.
    pages cm
  ISBN 978-1-58394-866-8 (paperback) — ISBN 978-1-58394-867-5 (e-book)
  1. Advaita. 2. Spiritual life. I. Title.
  B132.A3M78 2015
  294.5'44—dc23
  2014021819

1 2 3 4 5 6 7 8 9   VERSA   19 18 17 16 15 14

CONTENTS

2. SPIRITUAL PRACTICE

3. DIFFICULTIES ON THE PATH

EDITOR'S NOTE

This collection of talks was recorded at *satsangs* during retreats conducted by Swami Muktananda, who has read and revised the transcripts.

Many different topics are addressed during the satsangs, particularly since much time is given to questions from participants, but the guiding principle remains always the same and is identical to the teachings of the great masters of the past: "You are not this body, not this mind: you are the immortal, unchanging Self." It is the *"tat tvam asi"* of the Chandogya Upanishad, the *"aham brahmasmi"* of the Brihadaranyaka Upanishad, and the *"sarvam brahmamayam"* of Sadasiva Brahmendra. Swami Muktananda's entire teaching is aimed at leading us to this realization. To arrive there, however, requires a certain process of maturation.

The talks have been arranged to reflect the different stages in this process.

1) What is the true purpose of life? The answer given by the sages of India and other traditions is that we are here to realize God, which is to say, to become aware of our universal dimension and free ourselves from the illusion of being individuals confined within the narrow limits of our human condition. Chapter 1 deals with the direction we need to take and the mechanisms—particularly the egoic territory—that prevent us.

2) When the desire to set out on the path makes itself felt, certain practices are required. For many people this implies a reconciliation with the concept of "God." Questions about meditation, prayer, and various different techniques crop up. Answers to these are outlined in Chapter 2.

3) Once you are established in the practice, doubts begin to arise, created by the apparent confrontation between the spiritual path and the so-called real world, with all its conflicts and injustices. Responses to these are grouped in Chapter 3.

4) Chapter 4 deals with the need that participants often experience to fly to the rescue of other people, to resolve conflicts and restore justice. To what extent can we really help? How much can an individual actually achieve?

5) Identification with the individual we think we are is deeply ingrained and is particularly difficult to break away from in situations that concern us closely, especially our relationships, family, and work. In Chapter 5, Swami Muktananda invites us to change our point of view, not just during times of formal practice but at every moment of our lives, and to place ourselves on the level of "I Am," which is universal.

6) Everyone who wants to learn and progress needs a teacher, and this is particularly so in the spiritual sphere. In India, the tradition of transmission from teacher to disciple has been kept alive without interruption from its origins to the present day. In Chapter 6, Swami Muktananda touches on the relationship with a spiritual teacher through his personal recollections of his own teacher, Swami Chidananda.

7) Chapter 7 is devoted to awakening to the Infinite, to the "Spirit." It refutes our idea of being the body, overturns our concept of time and space, and dispels our notions of dreams and reality. It lifts the veil on our true nature, and when this is revealed the purpose of life is realized.

These topics are all closely related, and because some of the talks could have found a place in several different chapters, repetition is inevitable. The reader's indulgence is, therefore, humbly requested!

INTRODUCTION

Swami Chidananda: His Part in My Life

In early childhood, all that I, a French-speaking Canadian boy, knew about the spiritual path were the teachings of Christ, the words of the Old Testament prophets, and something of the lives of the Catholic saints whose biographies I had read in my grandfather's library.

When I was nine years old, my path crossed that of a great saint: Swami Chidananda. In the summer of 1969, my uncle and aunt, who knew Swamiji, took my mother, brother, sisters, and me to see him at Val Morin, north of Montréal. This first meeting is etched in my mind and I remember it as if it were yesterday: Swamiji got out of the car and came directly toward us children. My mother had bought a small box of raisins for me to give to him. He opened it immediately and with three fingers handed me a few. I tried to refuse with a wave of my hand—I did not like raisins—but he insisted. So I accepted and swallowed them whole. My brother, who loved raisins, also received a few. He tried to get more by putting out his hand, but with no luck. We were both frustrated: me because I disliked raisins and had to eat them anyway, and my brother because he liked them and had asked for more without success.

By the age of eleven I had already decided to dedicate my life to God. It was not until I was twenty, however, that I felt His presence within me like a great wave of inner peace. I was an engineering student at the time, doing work-experience in a small mining town in the middle of a forest. In the evenings, I used to go for a run through the forest, and while I was running a profound peace, which I knew to be God's, would flood my being. Soon afterward, I gave up everything for Him. I had read the words of Jesus: "Verily I say unto you, there is no man that hath left house, or parents, or brethren, or wife, or children, for the kingdom of God's sake, who shall not receive manifold more in this present time, and in the world to come life everlasting."[1] "Well," I thought, "in that case, I renounce everything for You!"

The aunt who had taken us to meet Swami Chidananda taught me to meditate in front of his photograph. One evening while I was meditating, I looked at the photo and said, "Why am I meditating in front of you? I don't even know you, and anyway it's Christ I want to see!" That night, Swamiji appeared to me. My body spontaneously prostrated before him, my face pressed against his feet, which I could see clearly. I felt his hands lift my head; he brought it up to his face and kissed me on the cheek. Then he turned and left. When I woke the next morning, I was still bathed in divine peace, and over the next few days I had several powerful spiritual experiences.

I was sure these experiences came from God, but a friend who shared my spiritual aspirations was unconvinced. He reminded me of the words of Jesus: "I am the way, the truth, and the life: no man cometh unto the Father, but by me,"[2] adding that the devil sometimes disguised himself as an angel of light. "How could a Hindu be an authentic spiritual guide?" he said. I replied that Jesus also said that if a man asked his father for bread, he would be given bread and not a stone—so how could my experiences come from the devil? And since all I asked from God was God, how could He betray me? In this way, throughout this first year, I was confronted by the demon of doubt, until I understood that the words of Christ refer to "I Am," to the stillness of your inner self, to your sense of soul, and not to the body of flesh and blood.

It was at this time that I discovered the teachings of Swami Sivananda, Swami Chidananda's master, translated into French by Jean Herbert. I was deeply moved by the teachings, which corresponded exactly with my own spiritual longing. I immediately began to follow the recommendations, rising at four a.m. every morning to meditate and, driven by the burning desire to realize God, spent all day in the awareness of His presence, inwardly reciting His name.

After five years of intense spiritual practice, the moment I had been waiting for arrived at last: Swami Chidananda was coming back to America, to

Maryland. How can I describe this second meeting and the weeks spent in his company? It was as if all the joys of the Christmases of my childhood had come together and been handed to me on a plate. Swamiji's presence radiated an aura of saintliness that pierced my soul and brought me untold joy. It was clear to me that he was a saint of Christ-like stature. I understood what Jesus's disciples and the companions of St. Francis of Assisi must have felt. Swamiji's every extraordinarily delicate gesture sprang from an awareness that was not of this world, and his penetrating gaze reflected the divine love in which he was anchored. Along with his other disciples, I followed him everywhere, as if I had always been part of the group. Before he left, Swamiji invited me to India, to the Divine Life Society ashram in Rishikesh. I spent nearly six months there in 1986 and had the privilege of serving Swamiji personally, while keeping up my spiritual practice and my job in the world.

Like most Westerners, I followed an academic and professional career. At nineteen, I enrolled at Polytechnique Montréal, an engineering college, and went on to study agroeconomics at the University of Laval in Quebec. In 1982, I started to teach high school math, physics, and chemistry, before setting up my own company in 1987. During this period I also visited several ashrams, in order to experience the monastic life. On November 14, 1999, Swami Chidananda invested me with the orange robe of a *sannyasi,* and I transferred the company to my mother and brother. I became a monk at the ashram of the Divine Life Society on June 2, 2000, a step that did not change my inner life since I had lived in the spirit of renunciation since 1980.

Throughout the years I spent with him, my relationship with Swamiji developed around two aspects: in one, he was maternal, indulgent, and attentive, even when I was not actually with him. In the other, he was a father who could be stern at times. The two aspects were complementary: the maternal relationship is a tangible expression of the inner life—empathetic, patient, and loving—while the paternal relationship curbs the egoic territory and forces the disciple to turn his gaze toward the Infinite, toward the divine Father.

In his relationship as the father, Swamiji never spoke, but resonated in me with the sweetness of the divine ocean. Ultimately, the father was an ocean of love, whose severity was just an appearance. My early relationship with Swamiji gradually gave way to the dimension of Being, where we are all one, where there are no "others."

There are several stages in the development of inner life, which include a certain leaning toward interiority, a period of ripening, as well as the desire to live on the human plane. But Being is different; it concerns the transcendent, what lies beyond the world. You could say that there is God-the-Mother who symbolizes inner life, and God-the-Father who represents awakening to the Spirit, to where you are one with the Infinite. In his attitude toward me—which was a lesson in itself—Swamiji encouraged me to turn away from the world and look toward the Infinite. This was the culmination of his teaching.

Swami Chidananda left a final message with his disciples: "I have done my duty, I have given you Gurudev's[3] message. Take it, and may God bless you." His entire life was spent as a disciple in the service of Swami Sivananda, whose teachings he spread until the end of his days. This was the example he bequeathed. He has been the shining ideal in the forefront of my life, informed by the light of my childhood religion. The purpose of this book is to share the teachings I received from Swamiji.

—*Swami Muktananda*
Rishikesh, 2014

1.

A FEW BASIC PRINCIPLES

RENDER TO GOD THE THINGS THAT ARE GOD'S

Throughout the ages, the sages of India have never ceased to proclaim the following message: "You are divine; you are not this body of flesh and blood; you are the immortal Self; you are an ocean of absolute knowledge and beatitude. Realize this and be free."[1]

Sages from other traditions have expressed the same truth. In Judaism, the Lord declared, "I am returned unto Zion [the subjective witness] and will dwell in the midst of Jerusalem,[2] and Jerusalem shall be called a city of truth."[3] These three stages describe exactly the three main steps to wisdom: first, draw the vital forces of life into your inner self; second, dwell in the holy city of "I Am," in the presence of God; third, awaken to the truth, which is to say, to the Holy Spirit that you are. Jesus was born a Jew, lived as a Jew in accordance with Jewish tradition, and died as a Jew. When he declared, "I and my Father are one," the Jews cried blasphemy and stoned him. Then Jesus said, "You are gods,"[4] meaning that what was true for him was true for everyone. This was his highest teaching.

In the Muslim tradition, Sufis chant the name of the Lord, which is also a widespread practice in India among those who want to realize God. These seekers remain absorbed in inner stillness, ripening in their interiority until, in the depths of the experience, they find "I," the divine Spirit. In this inexpressible state, they affirm "I am He" or "The Lord our God is one Lord"; in other words, "God Alone Is."

Life comes to an end, both for the billionaire who wields great power in the world and for the poorest of the poor who is shunned by all. The end of the journey is the same for everyone: this world draws to a close. When the body dies, what is left of your human characteristics? Can you take your nationality with you to the grave? When you are dead, to whom are you going to say "I'm an American, Frenchman, or Chilean"? Definitions have, of course, their part to play and must be given their due, but they nonetheless belong to the realm of the unreal.

The light in you is what knows, for example, that at midday it is daytime and that when night falls it is nighttime. The part of you that knows is not in the past or future, it is in the here and now. Eternity is in the here and now. The sages of India call it *chit,* or Consciousness. Consciousness, together with faith and love, are the powers of the light of the Eternal, of the divine Spirit, and you are that light.

Wherever you, the Spirit, place your belief, wherever you invest your power of love, takes on a quality of eternity. If, for example, you invest the light of your belief in your relationship with your mother and father, you believe that this relationship will last forever. Or if you believe "I am French," depending on the intensity with which you cling to the concept, you may believe that you will be French for all eternity. It is because the light with which you believe is eternal that you endow the concept with a quality of eternity. But the external world in which you have invested your light is not eternal. The worst form of idolatry is to endow something mortal with the quality of immortality. This is why it is important, in the first instance, to distinguish the real from the unreal and to invest your power of belief and love in the real. "I Am" is what is real in you.

The concepts in which you believe take on an artificial quality of eternity because you sustain them with your light. This is why you say of this temporary instrument, the human body: "I am a man" or "I am a woman." In a few years' time this body will be buried or cremated, so why is it that even though we know that people die every day, we still go on believing that we are the body? The solution is to give back to God the things that are God's. When God told Moses to go to Pharaoh and bring the children of Israel out of Egypt, Moses said, "When they ask me who has sent me, what should I say?" God replied, "Thus shalt thou say 'I Am' hath sent me unto you."[5] Since God Himself defines Himself as "I Am," practice believing that this inner realm of peace and silence, this feeling of "I Am" within you, is God. It is sacred, hallowed ground, and it is there that you must direct your light.

Compared to this sacred realm, every name and form, the whole of time and space, the entire creation, is nothing but a puff of smoke. This worshipful reality is the way, the truth and the life, through which all must go in order to return to the Father.

THE PARASITIC ATTITUDE

The measure of whether you are on the right path is the feeling of happiness that begins to arise in the background of your life. You had forgotten this happiness, yet it was there in the very first months of your life. A baby only has to pat a rattle hanging above its cradle to explode with joy. It is not pretending to be happy, it does not have to force itself, it is expressing true joy. The sound the rattle makes creates a wave of happiness that reveals the ocean of bliss that is the baby's very nature, the very nature of everyone.

The right attitude in life is to let yourself be lived and, as life in its different forms unfolds, to allow the fullness of your being to be revealed to you. Instead of this, we behave like parasites. Are you familiar with the parasitic mushroom? It is a type of fungus that grows on tree trunks, living off its host plant and giving nothing in return. It is so deeply embedded that it is impossible to dislodge with bare hands while the tree is still alive. Once the tree has rotted, the fungus moves on. Human beings have a similar attitude toward the world. When people go for a walk, for example, they look at nature and think, "I am the eye that sees the beauty of the light through the trees, I am the nose that smells the scents of the forest, I am the ear that hears the birds sing." They feel "open" and happy. They think their enjoyment comes from the scenery and when the walk is over they close up again and their joy evaporates.

That is fine, even inevitable; but you can do so much more than spend your whole life identified with sense organs and seeking pleasure in sense objects. Sense organs are impermanent; sooner or later they decay and die. But the human body, this temple, has the immeasurably more valuable potential of allowing you to discover your true nature: the state of wholeness, of plenitude. It is because people identify with their human aspect that they behave like parasites.

When you make room in your life for Life, and acknowledge the universal in you, you realize that the beauty of nature is part of inner stillness. On my way here this morning, a ray of sunshine was playing through the branches of the trees, lighting up the carpet of golden leaves on the ground. It was magnificent! That beauty, that moment in time and space, is contained in God in the form of "I Am." It is not separate from me and, like the baby's rattle, reveals to me the plenitude that I am. When you live with this attitude, it is not that you reject the senses, but you no longer regard them as the source of happiness.

It takes time to throw off the parasitic attitude, because the idea of being a person whose happiness depends on senses organs and sense objects is as difficult to dislodge as the fungus on the tree. People in whom this attitude is deeply embedded think, "But if I give up the enjoyments of life, what will I get in return?"

The following story from the Puranas illustrates this mindset. Indra, king of the gods, had insulted a sage and as a punishment was sent to earth in the form of a pig. Eventually, Lakshmi, the divine Mother, took pity on him. "Poor Indra!" she thought. "What a sorry state he's in, having to eat just any old rubbish." So the divine Mother came down to earth and went to see the pig, who had forgotten his true identity.

"You are not a pig," she told him, "you are Indra, king of the gods, master of nature, ruler of the heavens. It's sad to see you in this state. Why don't you come back to paradise with me?"

"That's very kind," said the pig. "I don't know. I'll have to ask my wife first."

When Indra told his wife about the divine Mother's offer, she hesitated. "Mmm, they're asking us to go up there, are they?" she said. "We ought to find out more about it before we decide. At least find out whether there is human excrement [which is what the pigs in India feed on] in paradise."

"You're right," said Indra, "after all, we're fine down here with our children, and there is plenty for us to eat."

Indra went back to the divine Mother and said, "We'd like to know whether there is human excrement in paradise?"

"No, of course not!" cried Lakshmi, horrified. "How disgusting! There is nothing but the purest, highest-quality nectar."

"Well," said the pig, "in that case, my wife and I are not interested!"

Believing that happiness can be found in gratification of the senses is just as primitive and repugnant as Indra's belief that happiness lay in eating human excrement. This is evident once you have discovered the source of your being.

Q: Then why have we been given sense organs?

A: Do you really have them? Are they really what you are?

Q: As a human being, yes!

A: Which of your senses are you?

Q: They are part of my body. I have eyes, ears, etc.

A: So you believe that they are what you are?

Q: They're solid. . . .

A: Yes, there is a certain solidity, and you, who are the light, have chosen to believe that your eyes, nose, mouth, and the rest of it, are what you are? At the moment, you can see the trees through the window, but can you guarantee that in two seconds time you will still be able to see them?

Q: No.

A: So they are not what you are. The faculty of sight is temporary. Are the faculties of smell and touch yours? Are they really you?

Q: No, but why shouldn't I make use of them?

A: That is not what I am saying. There is a time for using them and there is nothing wrong with doing so. What I am emphasizing is that it is not an end in itself. Sexuality, for example, has become the absolute criterion for human happiness. It has been made into a false god and is held up as the ultimate road to happiness. A man of seventy said to me the other day, "I can't stand getting old! I try to make love and can't. I still feel desire, but it doesn't happen anymore!" As we age, our capacities gradually decline and we do not have the same sexual potential at forty or sixty years old as we do when we are twenty.

Q: The same goes for everything; you enjoy eating one way when you're twenty and another when you're thirty. There are things you like listening to at twenty and it's quite different when you're fifty.

A: Yes, human beings evolve in time and space, but there is a world of difference between someone who has made room for interiority and someone who lives only for the external world. A young man in his twenties who

5

has made God the purpose of his existence can make love to his wife every day—it is natural at his stage of life. But as he grows older, as his inner world ripens, the current of his life that is directed toward the Infinite grows stronger, while the current directed toward exteriority, toward gratification of the senses, grows weaker. But this same young man, had he lived exclusively for the outside world, would experience the same desire in his eighties as he had in his twenties, because the current of his life flowed outward. The fungus was firmly embedded! This parasitic attitude prevents you from discovering the plenitude that you are because it makes you look in the wrong direction.

Until the day we die, society encourages us to be parasites. It tries to make us believe that we are our eyes, nose, ears, mouth, and so on, but all evidence points to this being false, since these faculties decay and die. You may persist in investing sense objects with a quality of eternity and seeking happiness there, but one day, when you are older, you will have to face the truth and realize that you have been looking in the wrong direction. This will be painful—and it will also be too late. When you reach the end of your life and have clung to the idea that happiness can found in the outside world, you die with unfulfilled desires and these generate yet another dream.

Q: But it's also thanks to sexuality that life goes on. . . .

A: And that death, rebirth, and the dream go on! Ever since the amoeba stage, reproduction and, therefore, sexuality, have always existed. But is that where true happiness has ever been found? Animals in the wild live in harmony with "I Am" and their environment is in a state of equilibrium. It is humans who live disconnected from life and, by blindly seeking to satisfy the senses, have created an imbalance. Look at the state of our planet! It is from this mirage that you are invited to escape. Through birth after birth, nature has evolved and created the human form that gives us the opportunity to recognize "I Am" and awaken.

Q: So is it about choosing to use your energy in a different way?

A: No! It is about choosing to be in a different way. You talk about using "your" energy, but the path of awakening is not about manipulating energy. Your identification with sexuality and your belief that happiness is to be found in sexual relationships have created an egoic territory, a false "you," which

6

is struggling like the devil in holy water to survive. But sexual energy is merely "on loan" to you for a limited period; you do not own it.

Whenever you attend one of these retreats, you will be encouraged to change the direction of your life and seek the answer to the question "Who am I?" Once you have set yourself this goal, and with the help of a different kind of understanding, everything you do can be spiritual. The actions of someone who follows this direction in life automatically become wise.

Human beings think they are civilized, but spiritually they are still in the Middle Ages, when the world was thought to be flat and people believed that the stars, sun, and planets revolved around the earth. Today, people think that everything revolves around them, which is why they treat nature with such scant respect. Their only rule is, "me, myself, and mine."

Sages from every age and religious tradition invite us to return home, to make room in our lives for His peace and awaken to the truth. But how many people are really interested? The vast majority has always turned down the invitation, it is nothing new, and if you decide to turn it down you are part of the norm. But if you decide to accept it, that is exceptional! When God told Moses to lead the people to the foot of the mountain and worship Him, what happened? They grew restless, and their most base desires soon came to the fore: "The people sat down to eat and to drink, and rose up to play."[6] What do people usually want? "Sex and drugs and rock 'n' roll!" The people came to God at the foot of the mountain, and even though they had seen the Red Sea part, even though they had been given proof of the authenticity of Moses's message, they made an idol of a golden calf and danced around it. God tried, but to no avail. Once the parasitic attitude has taken hold, it does not let go easily.

The human body is a difficult gift to obtain; it is a spiritual Lamborghini. But you are not this body; you are simply passing through it. The body is a catalyst that enables you to awaken to that which transcends this cosmic dream. It allows you to drink the water of life and awaken to the Spirit that you are. This is why sages invite us to make good use of this precious gift. It is up to you to think, weigh, and compare, and then to decide on your priorities.

Given that plenitude is your nature, happiness is a necessity in life. Sense organs are there to help you find it, on condition that you do not lose sight of the fact that plenitude cannot come from the stimulation of a few nerve endings! Many sages in India have lived a family life. As they advanced in age, they renounced sensual pleasure and anchored themselves in the Infinite. It is the same as when you spend a day at the beach: when you set off you are weighed down by many things, but as you get closer to the sea, you drop what you do not need and run into the waves almost naked. So, be happy! Take advantage of the pleasures that life has to offer, but not as a parasite.

YASHODA'S VISION

One fine afternoon in Vrindavan, Krishna was playing in the garden with his friends when he suddenly picked up some mud and put it in his mouth.

"Krishna," his friends protested, "you mustn't eat mud! Spit it out at once!"

But little Krishna, who was very stubborn, flatly refused. His friends decided to call on a higher authority.

"If that's how it is," they said, "we're going to tell your mother!" and they ran off to the house where Krishna's mother, Yashoda, was preparing some curds. "Yashoda, Yashoda, come quickly! Krishna has put some mud into his mouth and won't spit it out."

Yashoda, who was used to her son's tricks (she had been on the receiving end of them often enough), dropped her utensils and strode off to find him. "Krishna! What's this I hear? Now you're eating mud? That's no way to behave!" Unmoved, the child denied it.

"He's lying, Yashoda," his friends insisted, "believe us, we saw him!"

Not knowing whom to believe and wanting to be sure, Yashoda ordered Krishna to open his mouth. He obeyed, and when Yashoda leaned over to look into her son's mouth she was awestruck: she saw the whole of her village, Vrindavan, and its surroundings. The vision faded and in its place she saw the earth, sun, and planets revolving in the vastness of the firmament. Again the vision faded and the Milky Way appeared, followed by billions of galaxies and then the entire universe, including Yashoda herself peering into Krishna's mouth. Overcome, Yashoda started to tremble. At that moment, the vision vanished and everything returned to normal.

The Lord had revealed to Yashoda that the universe is an organic whole, of which "I Am" is the substratum. "Bala Krishna," the divine child, represents our inner self. Time, space, and the entire cosmic universe are an infinitesimal expression of God in the form of "I Am." Every night when you dream, a drop of "I Am" takes the form of the stars, earth, and the natural world. All His manifested forms are there in your dreams, including the person you think you are, with your apparent individuality.

People believe, "I am an individual. I am the one who acts. There is me and there are other people." Yashoda's vision reveals that in reality everything happens within "I Am." When Krishna denied having eaten the mud, he was demonstrating that it was "I Am," or life, that had acted. Eating, drinking, seeing, breathing, walking, thinking—any action whatsoever is done by life and not by the idea we have of being a name and form.

By abiding in the presence of God, you ripen in His peace. As it fills your being, you become the body of His peace and not a body of flesh and blood. This is the true meaning of Communion. And then, like St. Paul, you can say, "I live; yet not I, but Christ liveth in me."[7] The attitude that should underlie all our actions should be: "It is not I who sees, hears or thinks: it is Christ." When you put this into practice, the divine Spirit in you awakens.

SERVING GOD

The only thing you can really know, the only thing you are really close to, is your sense of being. You know you exist. You know no object in the world in the way that you know "I Am." You can see, smell, taste, or touch an object, but the knowledge you derive from sensory experience is of a different order to your sense of being.

As far as you are concerned, you are the one and only subject in the world and everything else is an object. You can say to an ant, "You are small and insignificant. I'm big and strong and I have the right to tread on you." But from the ant's point of view, it could say, "I'm the subject around here; get out of my way, you great big lump!" The sum of the experience of all those who consider their subjective truth to be the only valid truth is contradicted by the sum of the experience of every individual who sees "other people" as an objective reality. Who is right? An ancient rabbinical text states that Israel is at the center of the world and that Jerusalem is in the center of Israel. In Hebrew, "Israel" means "he who sees God," i.e., "I Am," and in this context it refers to the human being. The word "Jerusalem," which is made up of *jeru*, "fear," and *shalom*, "peace," refers to "I Am." But in Hebrew, the word "Jerusalem" also contains the idea that if you are on the inside, all is God, and if you are on the outside, there is nothing. So when you are in communion with "I Am," there is only God. But if you identify with the world of concepts, with the belief that you are in "France" or "America," there is nothing.

What I put to you now is that peace, inner stillness, interiority, is what God is, and this implies a dignity of belonging to the divine. It is not a concept, an idea in your head: it is a fact. And if I realize that the stillness in me is God, I have to acknowledge that each and every one of you is part of it, that everyone is automatically included. My attitude toward you will be conditioned by this realization and I will not, therefore, behave in an egotistic manner. What makes the difference here is that I invest my faith as prescribed by the sages of India, by the Old Testament, and by Christ.

When Moses arrived at the foot of the mountain, God ordered him to summon the people so that they might serve him. To serve God is to recognize that "your" inner peace is a sacred place, that it is God's realm. If you live in communion with His presence, you realize that everything in existence belongs to Him in the form of "your" inner peace, which is none other than His peace. In this way, the peace of the Almighty descends on earth and you become its servant. The Spirit that you are is then revealed to you.

But how many people are interested? When the people arrived at the foot of the mountain, they set about having a good time. Who wants to awaken? The vast majority of people are not interested in this message. There is nothing new under the sun.

THE DEER

Just like deer that give off a strong scent and run around wondering where the smell comes from, human beings spend their lives running around searching for happiness in the world of objects.

The secret is to learn to find happiness in the stillness of your inner self, in "I Am," and to realize that there you have your best friend, your greatest support, because that which is present in you in the form of interiority is God. Be happy in this presence, unburden your problems and even get angry if it helps, but learn to be content in the space of your inner being. This space is often wrongly interpreted as one of sorrow, loneliness, or fear, but in fact it is there that you find supreme happiness, and it is there that the Infinite and the Spirit that you truly are abide. "That which is night to all beings, in that the self-controlled man is awake; when all the beings are awake, that is night for the sage who sees."[8]

THE BIRD AND ITS REFLECTION

Does the ego really exist? Do human beings really have an ego? The following anecdote throws some light on the question.

The glass-paneled doors of the satsang hall at the ashram in Rishikesh are tiled on the inside and from the outside look like mirrors. Four years ago a little bird came and perched on the bars of the door. Fascinated by his own reflection, he sat there chirping away all day. Can you say that a bird has an ego? Of course not! But this little bird believed in the reality of his reflection and could not stop looking at himself, convinced that what he saw would bring him happiness. After a while, Mrs. Bird arrived (recognizable because she was more delicate and appeared to be wearing eye makeup). To begin with, Mrs. Bird pecked angrily at Mr. Bird, calling out shrilly as if to say, "What are you doing here, you stupid idiot! Come on! Come home!" This sent Mr. Bird into a rage and, flapping his wings furiously, he screeched, "Leave me alone!" then immediately returned to the object of his passion: his reflection in the mirror.

Anger is the first symptom of what can be called the "egoic territory," which follows universal laws. The bird was convinced that what he was doing would bring him happiness and he was determined not to let anything get in his way. Furious with his mate, he grew increasingly loud with his squawks as he beat his wings as if to say, "Who asked your opinion? Mind your own business, go away and leave me alone!"

Every creature in nature is searching for wholeness, for plenitude, because plenitude is what we are. But because we look for it in the wrong direction, we often cannot "see" what is right and we get diverted from our true path. Blinded by desire, we then take refuge in anger, criticism, and self-justification.

As far as our friend the little bird is concerned, matters have now improved and he no longer spends all day perched on the door. When Mrs. Bird arrives she seems resigned to having a lunatic for a husband and sits quietly beside him as though doing her knitting. Mr. Bird appears to have grown up a little and is less interested in his reflection. (And luckily there is no divorce in the bird world!)

More or less the same thing happens on the human plane. In reality, human beings no more have an ego than do birds. The ego is a ghost, created by the belief that someone or something belongs to you. This belief leads to "my" children, "my" house, "my" country, "my" religion, "my" opinion, and so on, which in turn gives rise to an egoic territory. There is no single ego, but many potential egoic territories. As with the bird, the world is a mirror that continually reflects the names and forms with which we identify in the mistaken belief that they will fulfill us. Our error is to forget that our true nature is beatitude. The Spirit is plenitude and you are That.

IF I GAVE YOU A PALACE

If I gave you a palace, a Rolls Royce, and a pile of gold, but on the condition that you had to live on a desert island, you wouldn't be interested, would you? This demonstrates the true value of things. If a man is driving a Rolls Royce, people will look at him admiringly, kids will point and say, "Look at that Rolls!" and the man, cigar in hand, thinks, "Yes, that's me" (while pretending not to have seen them). It is you, the passerby or child, who validates the man's idea of himself. For whom is the Queen of England queen? Only for those who believe in her—you don't see animals bowing down before a throne!

It is you who create the world by mistaking the definition of things for reality itself. The idea "I am poor" leads to the idea "if I get rich, I'll be happy." The idea "I am ugly" leads to "if I were handsome, I'd be happy." The idea "I am this or that nationality" leads to a whole range of ideas you do not need me to spell out! In this way, because you invest love, the light of your soul, in the wrong place, a mountain of concepts and egoic territories form and crystallize.

No one can live without faith. Your beliefs determine your religion, and today religion consists of sex, power, and money, on whose altars anyone rich and famous is envied and worshipped, be they pop singers, movie stars, football players, or politicians. These people must have prayed throughout many lives to have accumulated all the things they have. But what do they really have? They have achieved their idea of fulfillment, and yet are most of them satisfied? Do they say, "Thank you, God, now I have all I need. I want nothing more"? No! They are still unsatisfied.

I have been to the poorest countries on the planet, but the biggest beggar I ever met was a billionaire whose family owned a large company. This billionaire also owned a major baseball team that, year after year, failed to get into the finals. One season, however, the team won enough matches to have a chance of reaching the final series, but it then lost five matches in a row and had to abandon any hope of qualifying. I was having dinner with the owner on the night of the fifth match. He was depressed and in a furious temper. In spite of all his power and vast material wealth, he was still saying to God, "Please give me more!"

When people are alone, whether they live in a castle or a hovel, own a yacht or a dinghy, are as rich as Croesus or crippled by debt, they usually interpret inner peace and silence as loneliness. There is no one around to validate their self-image. In an attempt to escape the intolerable burden of inner peace and silence, they turn to drink, drugs, or other forms of gratification that lead to every sort of physical and mental suffering. This eventually forces them to recognize the importance of making room in their lives for interiority—if it is not too late.

The whole universe, including space and time, is but a speck of dust compared to the Infinite that is in you. When you realize that on the inner plane you are heirs of the Almighty, you are at home wherever you are. At the level of inner reality, everything is yours and nothing is outside you; there are no "other people." When you stop believing in the outside world, it loses its attraction. Humans are like children playing in a sandpit: when they have had enough and start to cry, their mother quickly comes to find them and takes them home.

THE EGOIC TERRITORY AND ITS LAWS

Every attribute of "I Am" can potentially create an egoic territory, and where there is a territory there is an army to attack or defend it.

The idea "I am a man," for example, defines a territory with a life of its own that belongs to the world of multiplicity, of names and forms, whose laws are exact and scientific. Actions that spring from the egoic territory "I am a man" are conditioned by the degree to which you are invested in the idea of belonging to body and mind. In extreme circumstances, and depending on the degree of spiritual evolution, an intense attachment to body and mind can lead, for example, to someone committing rape. There is no need to single out criminals here: we have all seen how at a party even normally law-abiding people are capable of such acts. We are all capable of such acts; it depends on how we invest our light.

The current of life can flow in two directions. *Vidya maya,* the current that flows from the world of multiplicity toward interiority, carries you back to the Infinite. The opposite current, *avidya maya,* draws you into the world of multiplicity and is sustained by the concept of a personal "I," as in "I am this or that attribute." It is this current that produces ignorance and a lack of awareness

You are an ocean of bliss, but the notion of individuality, the "I-thought"—as Ramana Maharshi, the great sage of Arunachala, called it—creates a need, a sense of incompleteness. The urge "I want" then arises and produces a negative to complete the positive. The idea "I am a man" spontaneously produces "I need a woman." There is nothing wrong with this; what is wrong is to remain trapped in the identification. The *sanatana dharma,* your eternal duty, is to make room in your life for God's presence and to ripen in the peace of the Almighty, and not in this mortal body of flesh and blood with a mind filled with thoughts.

The behavior of people who identify with exteriority is predictable: two people at the same level of spiritual evolution and with the same crystallization will, in similar circumstances, behave in a similar way. But the actions of people who identify with interiority are never predictable, because their actions are born of the intelligence of the Infinite. When the Infinite expresses itself, every expression is unique; snow falls but every snowflake is different.

Jesus said, "Render unto God the things that are God's."[9] How should we understand these words? "I Am" is God, but people seize hold of "I Am" and bury it under a mountain of concepts. A wise person with faith no larger than a mustard seed tells the mountain to throw itself in the sea and the mountain instantly obeys.[10]

THE PSYCHOLOGY OF DESIRE

In what do you invest your power of belief? You are what you believe. If you believe that you belong to duality, you will always feel incomplete, because at any one time you can only ever be one half of a duality. This creates a want, a need, and makes you look for fulfillment in the external world of objects rather than in the subject, in your inner world, which alone is real.

If, for example, you are firmly attached to the concept of being a man or a woman, what do you desire? As a young woman put it to me frankly the other day, "What I want is a house and a man." Implicit in the concept "I am a man" or "I am a woman" is the "I-thought," which creates our sense of individuality. The individual experiences "I Am," or interiority, as boredom or loneliness, and this same "I Am" then becomes an impersonal, natural force we call desire. The human aspect of a man has certain physiological, psychological, and emotional needs, and when these become involved with the human aspect of a woman, the intolerable burden of inner silence is temporarily swept under the carpet.

When a man and woman get together, if their needs are satisfied, the wave of desire subsides and they taste a drop of fulfillment. It is with this drop that we experience human love, which lasts as long as each party satisfies the other. But the human aspect is not all you are. Human love is partial, conditional, and often unreliable. Of course there is the romantic phase, the sudden *coup de foudre,* the passionate intensity of a Romeo and Juliet when young girls dream of finding their Prince Charming and vice versa. But even the most wonderful dream cannot bring you complete happiness, because the world of dreams is ephemeral and ends with death.

Human love has its rightful place but it is not an end in itself. By loving God and practicing abiding in His presence, inner peace ripens and divine love awakens. When you are anchored in the Infinite, all the glory and love that you ever desired in the dream world, or perhaps even tasted, seem futile compared to the glory of divine love. In a man-woman relationship, divine love can, however, gradually replace human love, like the morning sun that rises in the sky to reach the midday zenith. At that point, family life becomes a paradise on earth. The chains that bind us are forged by the idea that fulfillment can be found in this or that object, but true joy does not come from the pleasure derived from the external world, it comes from the "I" of your being.

The secret of success is to live a life dedicated to God, to the exclusion of everything else, because the roles that are yours to play in this cinema of life are all included in Him. The Bible states this clearly: "Trust in the Lord with all your heart, and lean not on your own understanding. In all your ways acknowledge Him, and He shall direct your paths."[11]

LIVING CONNECTED TO LIFE

Q: Were scientists—such as Pasteur, for example, when he invented the anti-rabies vaccine, or anyone else who has made discoveries that have benefited mankind—"doing" anything or were they unconsciously in "I Am"?

A: What is "I Am"? A wave on the ocean is nothing but water. Can you imagine a wave asserting its Atlantic origins and fighting against a Pacific wave? A world of waves that believe they are separate from one another? The world of waves has no reality: what is real is water. We behave like waves that take themselves for separate entities and think they belong to a specific geographical area and a collective history. "I Am" is the only reality.

So who is "doing" what? Your ability to do anything at all stems solely from the power of life and not from your idea of who you are. Whenever you say "I see," you imply that it is you who controls the absorption of a photon by the chromophore, you who focuses the light rays onto the retina, who absorbs and translates the electrical signals supplied by photoreceptor cells, who projects the inverted visual information and turns it the right way up. The same goes for your other senses. When you say "I live," is it strictly true? Do you control your heartbeat or your other organs? Are you the one who regulates all these complex processes? Then who does? The answer is simple: life does.

Acknowledging this in no way invalidates Pasteur's discoveries, which were the result of how he chose to direct his talent and ambition, both in his life as "Pasteur" and in previous ones. Life is like the cinema: it is because light is directed onto the images of a filmstrip that a movie is created. The attitude "I am the doer" traps you in the cosmic dream, while the attitude "God does everything" sets you free, even though your life situation may not change much. What was Pasteur's inner attitude? I don't know. That was between him and God!

Good deeds are a worldly person's virtue and that is as it should be. For a spiritual person, goodness is insufficient: only awakening to the Spirit of the divine Father is worthwhile, and it includes being at the service of fellow human beings.

THE INDIVIDUAL AND THE UNIVERSAL SOUL

Q: What is the soul in the Catholic tradition and how does it relate to "I Am"?

A: The sense of soul we feel we possess is "I Am." Christ said, "Render to God the things that are God's." As soon as you say "I am a man" or "I am a woman," you appropriate "I Am." Giving back to God what is God's is to acknowledge that your sense of soul, which you learn to recognize in meditation, belongs to God. Because God is one, the soul is universal. When God is present in the form of peace, unbounded by time and space, how can anything be outside Him? All is contained in Him and the entire universe is but a speck of dust compared to His peace.

Q: Nevertheless, in India there is a distinction between *jivatman*, the individual soul, and *paramatman*, the universal soul.

A: The jivatman exists so long as you have not recognized that only the paramatman exists. The sense of being a separate individual arises as soon as you qualify "I Am." Believing "I am a man" is enough to create an egoic territory in which there is the "I-thought." This gives rise to the feeling "I am a subject in a world of objects," or "I am an individual witnessing what is going on around me." It is precisely this sense of being a subject that experiences the soul, hence the expression *jivatman,* and it is with this sense of an individual soul that we are invited to realize God. As long as you identify with the human person, certain practices are necessary in order to mature.

The individual is like a wave that, when it realizes it consists of water, thinks "This is my water." But water is, of course, universal, and forms the essence of the billions of waves that play on the surface of the ocean. The metaphor is imperfect because the ocean is conditioned by space and time, but it illustrates how, when you abide for a long time in "I Am," you become firmly convinced, through interiority, of the fact of the existence of God. The universal nature of "I Am" is then evident: the jivatman, the individual soul, never really existed; there is only the paramatman, the universal soul.

The implication of seeing things from this perspective is important. If I, as a separate individual, look at a tree, I see it as an object outside myself. I immediately name it, judge it, and like or dislike it. "It's a pear tree" or "It's a eucalyptus," "It's magnificent" or "It isn't tall enough." This is the scientific approach (except for liking and disliking, since scientists are supposed to be objective). Scientists observe and classify objects according to their structure, function, physical characteristics, and so on, which limits them to the narrow framework of the subject-object relationship.

But what about Life that gives life to the tree? The answer to this question can be found only by turning within, which is to say recognizing that your subjective experience of interiority is God. And if God is there, in the form of peace, if everything is contained in "I Am," then the tree is also there, as is the sense of "me" and "you": we are all part of one and the same reality. An ecology of interiority founded on respect then arises naturally and, unless I have good reason, I will not, for example, cut down a tree or harm it in any way. The merest insect or blade of grass belongs to "I Am"—and love is present there.

Those who have the dignity of belonging to God in the form of inner peace live in harmony with God; this is true communion with the body of Christ. Those who see that all forms of existence, from the humblest to the greatest, share in the dignity of belonging to life, truly honor the commandment "Love thy neighbor as thyself."[12] Meditate deeply on this.

MOZART, THE MAN AND HIS MUSIC

In relation to the universe, human beings are no more important than a nest of ants. You are not this human person. When you arrive at the time of death and return to that mysterious stillness, what remains if you have invested all your belief in human beings rather than in inner peace and silence? Who remembers anyone who died a hundred years ago?

Q: That depends on what they did.
A: It's true that on Armistice Day, for example, official ceremonies are held to commemorate those who sacrificed their lives on the battlefield, but who remembers each individual buried under every cross?

Q: What about someone like Mozart?

A: What about him? His music is undoubtedly extraordinary, but as a person there was nothing special about him. His genius? If you look at the manuscripts of his music, you will see that he never crossed out; it is as if he directly transcribed the sounds he heard in his head. And where did those sounds come from if not from the stillness of "I Am"? Mozart's music was an expression, a modification, of silence.

Which is greater, Mozart's music or silence? After death, the soul passes through realms with music so subtle and sublime that Mozart's is nothing in comparison. Mozart's work and his genius are an infinitesimal expression of the Infinite, which is present here in the form of silence. You can listen to Mozart's music and enjoy it, but there is also a way of listening to it with your heart and letting yourself be touched at the source of the sublime music, where there is inner silence.

Nothing in the world of name and form should impress you. Mozart the person is only significant insofar as he made room in his life for Life and awakened to the truth. Genius is a tiny expression of "I Am," and if Mozart was endowed with musical talent it was because he had longed for it in previous lives. Once attained, the object of desire no longer holds any value for the person. Sooner or later, humanity will lose Mozart's precious music because everything in this world dies or disappears.

Your dream is shaped by whatever impresses you, and this in turn shapes the way you are. What effect does the concept "Mozart" have on you? What does it evoke? How does it affect the way you see the world we live in? Think about it. What effect does the concept "America," "France," or "Canada" have on you? How does it influence your self-image? Meditate deeply on this.

At every moment you invest the light that you are in what you believe. If you invest your light in the images of a dream, the dream is kept alive, just as a movie keeps running as long as light is projected on the filmstrip. Be careful where you direct your light! "Mozart" is just a concept. You make him into a god, but as the Quran states, "Your only God is God."

I love Mozart and his music, but for me they are both part of His peace; that is why the concept of "Mozart" does not impress me. The world of objects excludes the inner life, but the kingdom of which Jesus spoke when he said "My kingdom is not of this world" is interiority connected to God and it includes the world of objects. Abide there and you will become an instrument of His peace.

THE PURPOSE OF EVOLUTION

What is the purpose of the universe? Water from the sea evaporates, falls onto mountains as rain, and makes its way back to its source, the sea. The same goes for certain species: salmon, for example, undertake an enormously difficult journey to swim back to where they were spawned. The universe is an organic whole that is continuously returning to its origin, to "I Am."

The universe has evolved into a multitude of names and forms whose intelligence has gradually developed during the process. At the beginning there were stars, from whose dust our planet was born. After billions of years, life began and flowers and trees appeared. These forms contain a certain kind of primitive intelligence. If, for example, you connect a flower to a lie detector and place it near a flame, the instrument shows that the flower can detect the danger. Then the animal kingdom emerged, a highly intelligent life form characterized by the inexorable cycle of life and death, but it was always in perfect equilibrium until the arrival of a certain animal: humans, the source of so much disharmony.

In Genesis, Adam and Eve are banished from the Garden of Eden for having eaten the fruit from the tree of the knowledge of good and evil. The metaphor illustrates our particular position in the world as the first animal with the capacity to recognize that which gave birth to the universe, to recognize "I Am." A chimpanzee can be taught five hundred words in sign language but it cannot recognize "I Am." Animals share in the dimension of "I Am" and benefit from the bliss of the Infinite, but at best they cannot progress beyond the level of a two year-old child. For human beings, however, knowledge of "I Am" is the beginning of a long journey back to the Infinite, during which they have to undergo a great deal of suffering. As soon as they try to grasp "I Am," death becomes "their" death, pain "their" pain, a country "their" country, an idea "their" idea," and so on, and this is the origin of all human suffering.

Do not judge the world; each thing has its place. Nature does not belong to human beings; it is human beings, with all their madness, that belong to nature. Nature is an expression of "I Am," and the suffering that humans bring on themselves with their misdeeds is there to force them to turn toward that worshipful reality. We must live in the world as instruments of His peace, but we must also acknowledge that the world is as it is. It is an expression of His will and is, therefore, as it should be.

When you understand this, the sleeper in you awakens to Being. This cosmic dream, including time, space, and a multitude of previous lives, never happened. This is the purpose and end of evolution.

FEARS AND INTERIORITY

The human body is a spiritual Ferrari, yet most people are crawling along at one mile-per-hour—some are even going in reverse! But if you use the potential that the gift of human life has given you to realize God, don't be surprised to find that He manifests in your life in a tangible way; it is only natural. His strength protects and guides you. You are the sons and daughters of the divine, not of humanity.

Q: Yes, but it's frightening.

A: Ah! Fear, the big word!

Q: It's the fear of never getting there, of never making it.

A: You will never get there if you look for happiness in the world of name and form. Everyone who lives like that lives in fear.

Q: What is fear?

A: Fear is the Infinite exerting its pull on you. It is that place in you where you have a sense of vastness, of the unknown. There are endless reasons for feeling frightened but fear itself is always the same. The root cause of all fear is the fear of death and death's many offshoots: fear of losing a loved one, fear of losing your money, work, house, reputation, and so on.

Fear is not "your" fear: it is an inner current that flows toward God, to the Infinite that you are. Meditate on God, contemplate Him in your thoughts; it will bring you great joy and inspire you to make Him the purpose of your life. Nothing is more comforting. Look fear in the face and know that God is manifesting in you in the form of the current that carries you home. Have faith in Him. Let yourself be borne along by the current and you will discover what you really are.

HUMAN BEINGS ARE PART OF NATURE

Q: There are terrible people in the world who do terrible things, what should our attitude toward them be? Should we try to protect ourselves?

A: Have complete faith in God in all circumstances and abide in His peace. Let me give you an example. I was with a friend at the ashram one day when two foreign visitors came to see him. It is difficult to put into words the feeling these two men gave me; they seemed to give off a stomach-churning smell and it was obvious to me that they were murderers. What I felt had nothing to do with clairvoyance, "energies," or any other kind of fantasy. Their presence was unbearable and I left the room. My only protection was my trust in God, and that was enough for me. I know that the two men belonged to "I Am" and knowing this implies love, but that did not mean I had to stay around and make friends with them! This kind of situation shows that, over and above normal precautions, there is nothing you can "do" to protect yourself from anything.

The truth is that we ourselves have not always been good, kind, or spiritual. Throughout our progress in this cosmic dream, as we evolved from amoebas to human beings, we too have committed crimes; it is part of evolution on this plane of the universe. A man not yet at the spiritual stage of development and who is firmly crystallized in his identification with sex, for example, will inevitably, in a given circumstance, commit rape. In another part of the world, another man at the same stage of development and with the same egoic territory will commit the same act if he finds himself in the same circumstances. Why? Because at that level there is no free will. The men's behavior is dictated by what they believe in, and their belief is invested in a concept. But be careful! When you feel like judging someone because you think you could never behave like him or her, know that you are potentially what you judge, and that you too are capable of behaving in the same way.

Human beings have a tendency to look at the world as if they were not part of it, as if they were above and beyond it. Yet wars have always existed, and what do men do in time of war? They steal, rape, kill, and plunder—so what's new? I am not talking now from the standpoint of right or wrong, I am pointing out to you that human beings, with all their qualities and defects, are an integral part of nature, and as such, like all other creatures, are in the process of evolving. Eventually, the suffering we undergo as a result of our actions softens our hearts. There are sharp rocks on the seashore that cut your feet, but in thousands of years' time those rocks will have turned to sand. The same goes for the human heart: it is cruel and merciless to begin with, absorbed in "I want, I want, I want," but gradually, through wave after wave of suffering, it becomes gentle, patient, and kind.

One day the cosmic dream comes to an end and it is time to awaken. Why do you wake up in the morning? Simply because it is time to wake up. How can I judge anyone who is still sleeping when I myself was asleep not long ago? That is why it is better to refrain from judging anyone at all.

EUTHANASIA

Q: I find other people's suffering unbearable, particularly when it's someone close to me. I would so like to be able to help! My father is old and suffering mentally and physically. What is your view on euthanasia, when someone is in such pain that all they want to do is die?

A: Euthanasia is having a precious instrument in your hands and not knowing how to use it. People do not understand the beauty of life and they misuse it. We live in an extraordinary universe that we gaze at in wonder. Everything we discover, from the infinitely small to the infinitely great, is a source of amazement. We understand some of the universe's laws but for the most part it guards its secrets. We journey through vast, icy, interstellar space on this tiny planet Earth and yet we can touch, in our interiority, the principle that lies at the origin of all this beauty: life.

You must learn to let yourself be lived by life rather than just living. When you make room in your life for Life, you learn to trust it. There are times when I have been in bed with the flu, for example, and could not feel inner peace because "I Am" was manifesting in the form of illness. I used a meditation taken from the *vyahita-vidya*: "This certainly is an excellent penance or austerity when a man suffers due to illness; he who knows this verily wins a great world."[13] (The "great world" here refers to the Self, the Absolute, which can never be an object of perception to the mind.) Illness falls like rain and reveals the joy of the present moment; so let go and allow the divine Self to unfold. My attitude was: "Lord, may Your will be done and not mine. I am That on which illness has taken hold." This attitude is symbolized by the Cross: have absolute faith in God and live with the conviction "I am Thee." In this state, something joyous and oceanic arose in my consciousness and illness resonated like the "Ode to Joy" of some divine symphony.

Suffering is an expression of "I Am" manifesting in the world of duality, and is always the direct result of our selfish actions. Suffering is not there to make us unhappy; on the contrary, it is the expression of an infinite love inviting us to go back home. People who identify with the intellect loudly assert: "I'm in control. God is just an alibi for the weak, a screen to hide behind from the fear of death." But suffering returns again and again and forces them to turn toward God. Finally, after many thousands of lives, and when they have reached the end of their tether, they cry, "Help me, God! I want to go home." If they then hold onto the conviction "I and my Father are one" and abide in His peace, so long as they remain on the path, suffering goes out of their lives never to return. Its job is done.

This does not mean that we should rejoice in suffering or do nothing about it: we should do everything in our power to relieve it. But if we invest our belief and love in the idea that happiness comes from the external world, from the world of name and form—be it a relationship or anything else—we are generating storylines for future lives in the cosmic dream.

Suicide is the worst of crimes. The divine Spirit has given you the precious gift of life, a spiritual Ferrari, which is very difficult to obtain. It has given you the opportunity to awaken to the divine Spirit and regain the glory of the Infinite that is yours for all eternity. And then you, this temple of the divine, shoot yourself in the head? That is a very bad idea indeed!

THE PARAPLEGIC CHILD

Q: What happens when, for example, a child is completely handicapped after an accident? There is no future on the human plane, but is there still hope for development on the spiritual level?

A: Everything is continuously evolving toward the Infinite, so a certain degree of development is always possible. When the brain has been damaged, the capacity to engage consciously in spiritual practice is nonexistent; but there is, nevertheless, hope.

We believe that our faculties of memory, discernment, and reasoning are what we are, but it is not so. We could lose these faculties in a fraction of second and yet we would still be there. They are not, therefore, what we are. Although a paraplegic child cannot follow a spiritual practice, that part of him or her that can never be affected, the immortal, indestructible Spirit whose nature is love, still remains. The light of the Spirit is there and the child's capacity to love remains untouched. We become what we love. If you are the parent of a paraplegic child and you practice being in His presence with the conviction "I am one with God," your inner self is filled with His peace. Without being aware of it, by loving you, your child will be loving that space in you that is filled by God, and he or she will therefore be loving God.

Paradoxically, we have a tendency to believe that we have to "do" something in order to help. It is not so much our actions that count but our attitude. If you identify with the body of flesh and blood, your child will remain at that level, but if you recognize that your child has, like you, the dignity of belonging to God, you immediately realize that by serving your child you are serving God. Then your child no longer loves you as a person, but loves God through you. When the divine Spirit in you is revealed, when you are anchored in Him, you bear witness on earth to His presence. This is the greatest service you can render, the greatest force for transformation, and the highest prayer.

THE DEATH OF GANDHI

Mahatma Gandhi's whole life was turned toward God. He began the day with a prayer to Rama (one of the Hindu names for God), to Allah (the Muslim name for God), to Buddha, Moses, and Christ. He did this to emphasize that God is one. In the Hindu tradition, God is worshipped under many names and forms, and Gandhi felt himself to be Hindu, Christian, Muslim, and Jew. Martin Luther King, Jr., said that Jesus brought the light but it was Gandhi who showed us how to use it.

Gandhi lived his life according to the attitude that lies at the heart of the teaching of the Bhagavad Gita: "Lord, it is not I who do but Thee." This is not a passive attitude, as Gandhi himself demonstrated—no one could accuse him of being inactive—and although he advocated nonviolence he nevertheless played a decisive role in the world.

Gandhi died when someone fired three bullets into his chest. At the moment of death, your innermost self is revealed and you cannot hide what you have been in your life. When Gandhi was shot, the name of God sprang to his lips and he fell back chanting "Hai Ram! Hai Ram!" Had he believed that he was responsible for bringing independence to India and brokering a peace between Hindus and Muslims; had he believed that the two nieces of whom he was so fond, and who were with him when he died, were "his" nieces, do you think the name of God would have been on Gandhi's lips in the last moments of his life?

According to the Indian scriptures, if you die thinking of God, you go to God. At the moment of death, Christ received the glory of the divine Father and it was the same for Gandhi. Anyone who lives a life connected to God is invited to receive His glory.

AT THE HOUR OF DEATH YOU REAP THE REWARDS

At the hour of death, you cannot disguise how you have invested the light that you are; at that moment the mask you have worn all your life falls away. The Indian scriptures state that if you repeat the name of God when you are dying you realize God, and the dream that is drawing to an end will be your last. But it is not that simple.

Ma Anandamayi told the following story: A poor, elderly woman used to visit her neighborhood shop from time to time to beg for oil. "A little oil," she pleaded, "please, just a drop!" But the woman who ran the shop always refused, saying, "No, not even a drop!" When the shopkeeper was close to death, her children urged her to recite the name of God, "Mother, repeat Rama, Rama, go on, repeat it," but all the shopkeeper could say was, "Not a drop, not even a drop."

Because your actions are a direct consequence of whatever is occupying your innermost self, there is no free will. Let me give you an example.

Everyone has problems at work, and the interiority of people who have not made any space in their lives for God is entirely taken up by these problems. When they get home from work, even if they are with the people they love, their thoughts will be elsewhere. A man might want to be a "good father," he might be aware that he is not paying enough attention to his children and might try to make up for it, but his actions will flow from an inner self entirely absorbed with work and it will be the banker, departmental head, employee who is trying to improve his relationship with his family.

The human body is a precious gift that enables you to touch the presence of God. When you dive into the innermost stillness of your heart during prayer, all your problems become His problems and no longer yours. It is not as important to solve your problems as to have complete faith in Him. Just as the essence of every wave is water, so the essence of every name and form is the stillness of interiority. If you repeatedly return to this inner stillness, it eventually fills your being, and the crystallization that had formed because of your identification with body and mind begins to dissolve. Once it is well and truly dissolved, you discover that you are nonetheless still there. Through His peace, and your belief that you are one with Him, the Spirit in you, which is none other than the Holy Spirit, awakens. Where you are Spirit, there the Infinite is also. All you need to do is anchor yourself in the Spirit and bear witness to the truth.

If you have never paid a penny into your bank account, there will be nothing in it when your bank statement arrives. In the same way, if you do not make space in your life for the peace of the divine, you cannot expect your interiority to have matured when you arrive at the hour of death.

WHERE DO THE WORDS OF CHRIST COME FROM?

Q: Where do the words of Christ come from and how do we know them?

A: The words of Christ are in the here and now, in your heart in the form of peace, just as the words of the Indian sages have been since the dawn of time. All are an expression of the same truth. You discover this for yourself when you direct the light of your faith into interiority. That is where you find the inner truth.

For me, Christ is not just a man who lived some two thousand years ago: he is That from which my words arise at this moment and That which in you receives them. Christ is not just a historical person: he is alive in the here and now.

LETTING YOURSELF BE TOUCHED BY LIFE

You are here to "be lived," to let yourself be touched by life, and not just to live. There is a huge difference between the two. If you believe you are here just to live, then you are identified with the human plane, with the body and mind, and your world is limited to the external world. Whoever lives like this dies as a person, and for that person the dream of duality goes on. It is the wheel of death and rebirth. There is only one life, only one "I Am," but the light that you are has created innumerable dreams.

If, on the other hand, you let yourself be lived, let yourself be touched by life, then you are not a person, you are not this body. You are, in the first instance, "I Am," sacred ground; you are interiority touched by the events of life. And when you transcend interiority, *ananda,* the divine Being that you are, is revealed, whose nature is absolute bliss.

As long as you identify with the external world, you are living a dream. But instead of just living, you have the potential to recognize inner peace, to ripen in this peace and let it touch that part of you that is Infinite. If we were here just to live, we would also be here just to die. A life identified with the human plane ends with death, so what would be the point? You are not an individual, you are not a body of flesh and blood: you are the immortal Self. This is the most important lesson in life.

2.

SPIRITUAL PRACTICE

THE BASIS OF ACTION:
CHANGING THE DIRECTION OF THE CURRENT

One day, a man who had been following his own spiritual path for twenty years had a grave doubt: he wondered whether the direction he had been going in for so long was the right one. He heard of a sage living on a rock by the river. He went to him, and said, "Master, I've been following my own spiritual path for many years, but now I'm not sure I've been going in the right direction. Please give me some guidance."

"Go and sit by the river," replied the sage, "and tell it to flow in the opposite direction. If it does, you'll know you've been following the right path. If it continues to flow in the same direction, your practices have been in vain."

The man went and sat on the riverbank. Staring intently at the water and concentrating with all his might, he repeated, "River, change direction; river, change your flow." He kept this up all day but by nightfall the river had not changed course. The man returned to the sage and said, "Master, it didn't work. The river is still flowing in the same direction. What should I do?"

"You foolish man," replied the sage, "haven't you understood that the river in question is the river of your thoughts? You've been following your own spiritual path for many years, don't you know that your thoughts should flow toward the Infinite and not toward the external world? Your mind is a current of life, it doesn't matter which method you use, it must change direction; it must turn within and go back to its source, back to the Infinite. If you'd been following the instructions of a teacher all these years and had told your mind to change direction, it would have obeyed in the blink of an eye."

This story illustrates the attitude that should form the basis of all our actions, and it is the one advocated by the sages of ancient and present-day India. Avidya maya, the current of life that flows toward the external world, is made up of thoughts, sensory impressions, emotions, and memories, and is sustained by the powerful, impersonal drive, "I want." This drive lies at the origin of creation and is what enables us to create our own individual world. "I want" is there at every step, at every instant, and it is what keeps human beings trapped in the cosmic dream.

Once we realize that avidya maya takes us away from the source, we must consciously and decisively change direction and follow the other current, vidya maya, which connects us to our inner self, to interiority, and leads us to the Infinite. In vidya maya the mind is anchored in the knowledge that true joy and fulfillment can only be found in the divine. A wise person lives according to this belief and makes room in his or her life for interiority.

The essence of every name and form, the concept at the origin of all concepts, is "I Am." It is the state of the world before creation, before the Big Bang, before even time and space. "I Am" is the essence of the universe, just as water is the essence of a wave. Nothing can be separate from "I Am," any more than a wave can be separate from water. The principle "I Am" is life. It is a river, a current, which by its very nature flows to the Infinite Being. Only those who make room in their life for Life are truly living; those who live for the external world are not. Only those who are truly living are released from the bonds of karma and return to where they are one with the Almighty, where bliss is absolute. Then the cosmic dream in which they have been trapped for so long draws to an end.

THE BLACK VIRGIN OF MONTSERRAT

Not far from Barcelona, at the foot of the Montserrat mountains, lies the small village of Montserrat. Legend has it that about eight hundred years ago shepherds noticed a strange light at the top of one of the mountains. The light reappeared several days running, so they decided to go up and investigate. At the spot where the light was shining they discovered a cave, and in the cave was a beautiful black lady. In her right hand she held a sphere and on her lap sat a black child.

A statue was carved of this apparition and placed in a monastery just above the cave. After a while, the monks decided that the statue should be brought down to the foot of the mountain and a basilica was built in which to house it. The day arrived for the statue to be carried down in solemn procession on a palanquin, but when the bearers tried to lift it they were unable to raise it even an inch off the ground. Clearly the Virgin had no wish to leave the mountain! The monks accepted the message with humility and left her there, where she still is today.

When God manifests on earth, the message He sends has a profound mystical meaning. What does the cave of Montserrat symbolize? The cave of your heart. Why is the Virgin black? If you look into your heart, what do you see? Darkness, the unknown, a feeling of "I don't know," a sense of existence: the sense of "I Am." This feeling, this sense of the unknown, is Her, the most beautiful.

What does the world She holds in her hand represent? It symbolizes the entire universe, including time and space. If you recognize that your sense of interiority is Her, the most beautiful, then even a star five billion light years away is included in the here and now of "your" inner peace. Can you see that faith no larger than a mustard seed renders your sense of interiority sacred, and that it is then no longer "your" interiority but His peace? If your answer to the question is "yes," then you have understood how to transcend individuality. The entire universe is nothing but a ripple in the infinite consciousness of His peace. Since the whole universe is there in His peace, the human world and everything in it is also included, regardless of good and evil, likes and dislikes.

What does the child on the Virgin's knee represent? The practice of abiding in the presence of God and the ability to remain in that presence leads to a rebirth. The infant God on the knees of the divine Mother is you. When you love God in the form of His peace, you become the body of His peace because you become what you love. The infant is of the same nature as the Mother. God in the form of "I Am" is the Mother, the guide who leads us back home. My name for her is Mā. She is a concrete concept of God that enables you, as you mature spiritually, to abide effortlessly in His abstract peace.

Settle yourself comfortably in Her presence and let go. Mā spontaneously awakens you to the Spirit that you are. She frees you from past impressions and from the wheel of death and rebirth in which you have been spinning for so long, trapped by the idea that there is somewhere something in this world that can make you happy. It is so easy to be taken in by false gods!

Q: Does the top of the mountain represent the point where you awaken to God?

A: Yes. Why did the Virgin not want to descend from the mountain? We expect God to come down and talk to us at our level of identification. "I'm so-and-so's mother who never listens"; "I'm a shopkeeper and I don't have enough customers"; "I'm depressed and bored"; and so on. It is not up to God to descend to our level, it is up to us to climb the mountain of renunciation, to relinquish the mass of concepts and labels we attach to "I Am" and remain in a childlike state. True renunciation is to abide in "I Am," a state with few concepts but in which the world is yours. You are then at home wherever you are.

By abiding in the conviction "I am one with God," you dwell at the top of the mountain. When you live in the presence of God, His peace reveals to you where this conviction is true.

DIFFERENT LEVELS OF FAITH

At the beginning, your relationship with God is not unlike your relationship with a friend, and you talk to him as a friend: "Everything is in Thy hands, not mine."

After you have talked to Him in this way for a while, God manifests in your life in the form of peace and you recognize that this peace, which you feel in the depths of your being, is God.

While you ripen in the awareness of His presence, you awaken to love and realize that everything you had thought was real never really existed; it was all just a dream. There's no "other people and me," no "me and the world." All is Him.

These three levels are good, but the third is the highest. You usually remain on the second until you awaken to the third. You go back to the first when you are tired of the other two and feel the need to return to the human level. Each has its place, depending on the circumstances of the moment.

DEVAS

Q: What is a deva?

A: In Hinduism, devas are gods, celestial beings that exist on the subtle plane. Generally speaking, they represent the forces of nature: Agni, fire; Vayu, wind; and Indra, king of the gods, represents thunder, lightning, and rain. The Vedas, the ancient Hindu texts, codified strict procedures for the rituals and sacrifices that were performed to obtain the favor of the gods. When Krishna appeared, he declared that sacrifices and rituals were futile compared to man's potential for awakening to the divine Spirit.

Primitive devotion to gods, to the forces of nature, is natural for some people and can be effective, because devas are real forces of God manifested on the plane of duality. A farmer who makes offerings to the gods for rain to improve his crops may have his prayers answered. Some people light candles in church for sick friends or relatives—being a Christian does not preclude this kind of belief. If their prayers are answered, the believers thank God; if not, they feel betrayed and perceive God as cruel and merciless.

These prayers are all part of the dream. The relationship with God-as-you-imagine-him is a stage on the path to the truth and establishes the first contact between you and the divine, but to remain at this stage is not enough. The purpose of life is not to play around with the forces that sustain the dream but to awaken to the transcendental force of the universe, to the One, and bear witness to the Spirit.

If you want to be free, desire nothing, and all your needs will be met fully and spontaneously.

AWARENESS

Do you believe that everything you see, hear, touch, or think is reality? When you look out of the window, you see houses and trees, you hear cars go by and you believe that you are here, in Assisi. But this is not Assisi: it is your idea of it, a few impressions that have formed and set into a mental concept. Your concept of Assisi has no real substance. Similarly, "my" mother, "my" brother, "my" friend, "my" enemy, "my" house, "my" country, and so on, are just concepts that hold a special place in your heart because of the impressions these people or things have made on you. You mistake these outward relationships for an inward reality. What you call "society," which you believe to be real, is nothing but a narrow set of ideas you have formed about the things that concern you. They have nothing to do with the whole of your environment or with reality. If you live on the external plane only, you live disconnected from reality. Can you really call this "living"? What does "living" mean? Where is life in you? What are you pointing at when you say "I," if not to your heart, where you have a sense of "I Am"? That is where real life is. Do you have to undertake a long *sadhana,* an intense spiritual practice, before you can find it? No! Everyone has the capacity to recognize *in the here and now* the reality within. All you need to do is become aware of it.

Awareness is an act of the Spirit that you are. In order to awaken, you need to become aware of the totality of your surroundings and not just of certain objects. The sense of "I Am" is God, and God includes everyone and everything in time and space, over and above life and death, over and above the manifested and unmanifested. The practice of abiding in the presence of God ripens you in His peace, awakens you to awareness, and connects you to the "whole." Awareness is divine love and is revealed; it cannot be attained. The "whole" enables you to filter out false identifications and allows you, who are divine awareness, to shine in your true nature.

EDUCATING THE MIND

The mind is a collection of thoughts that flow in an unruly manner toward the external world in the hopes of finding happiness there. Mind is, by nature, undisciplined. In meditation, instead of being a slave to the constant movements of the mind, you learn to master them. Some thoughts, however, conscious or unconscious, are so deeply ingrained that they sustain the illusion that true happiness can only be found in the external world. Whenever the mind tries to pull you in that direction, train it to realize that what it is looking for on the outside is already within, in interiority. In this way your mind becomes your ally.

When you realize that objects of desire, whatever they may be, are but a tiny part of the Infinite, you feel *ananda,* absolute joy, arising.

DOES MEDITATION MEAN BELIEVING IN GOD?

Q: Meditation is considered a science, so do you really have to believe in God in order to attain the truth?

A: There is a school of thought that sees things this way, but it is not a view we share. Through meditation you can no doubt tune in to an inner reality and arrive at a very profound state, such as nirvana or samadhi. You can remain motionless in that state in a cave in the Himalayas for many years, but without the act of believing in God you do not even begin to touch the heart of the truth. As soon as you open your eyes, you are still the person who thinks it was *your* experience. Since you have not given up the idea of being a person, you remain bound to the world.

Truth cannot be attained; it is revealed to those who invest their love of God in "I Am" and who live with the dignity of belonging to "I Am." Truth reveals itself to those who live in communion with inner peace and practice believing that everything and everyone belongs to that peace. Meditation is important because it enables you to make room for His peace and incorporate it in your life. Meditation is part of the path, but the path is not the goal. In my own experience, in the here and now, the divine Spirit knows that God alone is and, for the Spirit that I am, there are no "other people."

The difference lies in what I believe about "I Am." If interiority is "my" interiority, then it excludes you and we are all separate from one another. If, on the other hand, I acknowledge the existence of God in my sense of inner self, then it includes everyone. If I believe that "I Am" is God, how can there be any room for "my" peace or "my" experience? When you practice recognizing this, you gradually awaken to divine love, which is the path that leads to the truth.

WHY WE NEED THE CONCEPT OF A PERSONAL GOD

At the beginning of spiritual practice, the concrete image you have of yourself requires a concrete concept of God to enable you to remain effortlessly connected to the abstract reality "I Am."

Every religion has different representations of God to guide its followers to the Eternal. In India, for example, Ganesha is the divine force that removes obstacles. From early childhood, Hindus are brought up with the myths and legends that surround Ganesha, who for them is unquestionably divine, and when they attend celebrations in honor of the god their hearts are spontaneously moved.

In my own village, Saint-Eustache in Western Quebec, we used to celebrate Christmas in the traditional way, in a big house that belonged to my grandmother. My brother, sisters, and I would meet up with our cousins and play wild games of hide-and-seek. We helped our parents decorate the Christmas tree and set out the crèche. After Christmas dinner there was midnight Mass, where we sang carols in praise of God and listened spellbound to the story of the birth of Jesus. It was a time of great joy, a time for God. Later, I was able to associate "my" interiority with Christmas Eve, which, like "I Am," is characterized by an absence of objects of the world, an absence of forms. And yet, what peace! What joy! I was able to feel that interiority *is* Christ.

The concept of a personal God allows you to let go and have a human relationship with His presence. Christ is your mother, father, child, friend, and beloved. Is it so difficult to be with your beloved? Relate to your personal God in whatever manner you find most natural and in this way you remain easily connected to the current of His grace, whatever commitments you might have at home or work. When a surgeon is carrying out an operation, he has to keep an eye on his assistants but their presence does not interfere with his work. In the same way, simple faith in the presence of God, your best friend, does not disturb whatever you are doing—on the contrary! While outward appearances may remain the same, a worldly person's home is in the world but a spiritual person's home is in His peace.

A NEW BIRTH

Q: Does our concept of a personal God have to be a person?

A: It depends on how you look at it. From one point of view the answer is no: how could God be limited to a person, any more than the ocean to a wave? But from another perspective the answer is yes, because the last obstacle to Self-realization is identification with the intellect, the subtlest of the mind's functions. Identification with the intellect makes you feel that the center of your being is in your head and that you have a separate, individual intelligence. Human intelligence is, in fact, the intelligence of the Infinite, refracted by the prism of your identification with body and mind. It is a highly sophisticated mechanism, no doubt, and unique to the human brain, but it is not what you are. If it stopped functioning—after a car crash, for example—the Spirit that you are would remain intact.

Begin humbly from whatever you identify with at the moment. As long as you identify with the person, the individual you think you are needs company so as to be able to remain effortlessly connected to God in the form of inner stillness; otherwise the "crystallized" individual grows bored and finds the apparent loneliness of interiority unbearable. When you practice being in the presence of God, His peace fills your being and you become the body of His peace. It is a new birth. Jesus said, "Unless one is born again, he cannot see the kingdom of God."[1]

Q: I grew up in a family of atheists and had no religious education. I feel no affinity with a personal God, but the path you propose speaks to me. Can I take "life" as my concept of God?

A: Certainly. But the question of "your" intelligence and "other people" then arises. "I Am" contains the intelligence of the Infinite and includes the whole universe. If your concept of "life" includes everyone and everything, regardless of your likes and dislikes, and if the idea you have of yourself can concentrate effortlessly on the concept "life," then that is fine. But can you?

Q: I think I've still got a lot of work to do!

A: To describe it as "work" means that you believe you are the one who is "doing," and in that case you do have to make an effort. The quality of spiritual life is determined by the amount of time you devote to God and His presence. What you experience as life as it is *is* God and God alone expressing Himself in you.

I suggest the following: sometimes you feel peace; know then that God is manifesting in you as presence. Sometimes you feel overwhelmed by thoughts and inner turmoil; know then that He is manifesting Himself in the form of absence. In either case, place your faith wholeheartedly in God. Allow yourself to be as you are. Look on God as a friend. And Swamiji is also here. How about it?

Q: That's great! Thank you, Swamiji.

CONCENTRATION AND MEDITATION

Q: What advice can you give about meditation? Should you meditate on a phrase, a statement, a name?

A: When you start out on the path of knowledge, you train your mind in the same way that you exercise your body. The principle is to focus your thoughts on a single object for a given period of time. Imagine a flower, for example, and say to your mind, "You're going to hold a mental image of this flower in the space between the eyebrows for a fixed length of time without thinking about anything else." This is a purely technical exercise in concentration that tells the mind, "You're going to do as I say and not as you want." Each time your mind escapes, bring it gently back to your object of concentration. Until now, your mind has been controlling you, but now you are learning to bring it under your control. The exercise reveals to you just how undisciplined the mind is: ask it to turn left and it turns right; it behaves as if it were an independent entity with its own agenda. This demonstrates that the mind, with which we so closely identify, can be observed as an object and is not, therefore, what we are.

The best time to meditate is between four and six-thirty in the morning, which means getting to sleep early! When you have made God the purpose of your life, meditation is a useful exercise to bring your vital energies back onto the path of His peace. Choose a representation of God, a poster of Christ in prayer, for example, and light a candle in front of it. Begin by concentrating on the image of Christ, shut your eyes and visualize the image in the space between your eyebrows. At the same time, feel yourself being filled by His divine presence. Imagine that the light of the candle is the light of His presence. Breathe normally and keep your face and body relaxed. Start with twenty minutes and gradually increase the length of time. Sustained concentration is meditation.

The name of God can also be an object of concentration. Repeating God's name and associating it with the feeling of His presence is the quickest, easiest, and surest path to ripen in His peace. It is the classic method of meditation, in which *tamasic* energy, which manifests as lethargy, and *rajasic* energy, which manifests as agitation, are replaced by *sattvic* energy, which manifests as inner harmony and equilibrium. Where the sexual drive is concerned, it is transmuted into spiritual energy, *ojas,* which is situated in the head and prepares the body to receive the descent of His grace, a process that requires strong nerves. It should be noted that once this transmutation has taken place, celibacy becomes effortless.

Meditation is necessary, especially in the beginning, but it is important to understand that as long as you are merely concentrating, your practice is simply developing your sense of "I Am," until this becomes a natural state that you recognize subjectively. It is not through the practice of meditation that you awaken to the divine Spirit but by putting your faith in "I Am." The path to awakening begins when you love and acknowledge the simple fact of the existence of God in "I Am." This is the river that carries you back to the divine ocean. "I Am" is, by nature, true meditation. All is His, All is in Him, All is Him. These profound truths are revealed by His grace, initially in the form of "I Am," and, when you have found "I," by the divine Spirit that you are. I repeat, these truths are revealed; they cannot be attained, and certainly not by the intellect, however great its powers of concentration.

On a practical level, these stages unfold effortlessly and spontaneously when with each breath you live with the attitude prescribed by the Bhagavad Gita, "It is not I who am doing, Thou art doing." When this is well established, you awaken to the Spirit. Classic meditation is no doubt useful because it can take you onto a subtle plane, but it is insufficient because it does not transcend the level of human intelligence.

Q: When the mind has been stilled by meditation, is that when you find "I Am"?

A: Not necessarily. Do you have to wait for the sea to be calm before finding water? When huge waves are stirred up by a storm, they remain water. "I Am" creates huge waves in the mind, and so what? "I Am" is present even when your mind is disturbed, and it is the nature of the human mind to be restless at times. But the mind is also the faculty that discriminates between the real and the unreal, between permanence and impermanence, between what changes and what is eternal. If you look inside yourself at this moment, do you have a sense of soul, a sense of your existence?

Q: Yes.

A: However simple it may seem, that sense of soul is "I Am," and meditation helps you to identify it. Remember that the entire universe is but a ripple of "I Am." The more firmly you anchor yourself in the conviction that "I Am" is "Christ," the more you are filled by great peace. Live with the dignity of "being Him" in the form of this peace. It takes time, practice, patience, and perseverance for this conviction to penetrate to the depths of your being, but once it has the false truths of the world no longer impress you, because the mountain of identifications with names and forms will have dissolved in the ocean of His peace.

Q: So it's how you apply your faith that makes the difference?

A: Exactly!

Q: But how can you remain in peace when terrorist attacks are taking place?

A: Throughout your life, various events are going to affect you at the human level, but from the standpoint that we have been discussing it is always "I Am" that is affected, and every event takes place within "I Am." Of course, things will happen that will cause terrible suffering, but you can either look at these events from a human perspective, with all the emotion and fear they give rise to, or you can see that the events are taking place within "I Am," and therefore, within yourself. Seen from this angle, they are not happening "over there" but here, in you. This is true prayer.

When you bring God into the equation, everything you encounter on your path is blessed. If you reduce the equation to the human level, with all its emotional reactivity, you cannot achieve much. By introducing "I Am," you are introducing something real: prayer, which is a positive instrument for peace. That is why when you adopt this attitude you render a service to everyone and everything and you become an instrument of His peace.

Q: Is that when emotion becomes compassion?

A: Yes.

Q: But doesn't compassion come from love?

A: The very nature of "I Am" is compassion and prayer. I was driving through Rishikesh one day when I saw a small puppy covered in sores limping along the road. I was on my way to an important meeting so I could not stop to help it, but because I recognized that the puppy was in me, in God in the form of "I Am," I immediately felt a compassion far greater than any human compassion, which was clearly of a divine nature. His peace, of which I was but an instrument, was of far more help to the animal that I could ever be humanly. In this way, life is full of opportunities to serve God at different levels.

But there is more. If I love God in the form of "I Am," and if I acknowledge that what gives life to the puppy is also part of "I Am," I have to acknowledge that the little dog and I are one. So, is there love? The answer is, clearly, "Yes." But if the dog and I are one, and there is, therefore, no "other," where is love? It is here, where you are! Yes, but where? There is no obvious answer to the question; you cannot hold love in the palm of your hand as you would an experience, because it is the very essence of the Infinite, the very essence of the divine Spirit that you are. And love is an act; it reveals itself at a point of being as the "I" in your life. It reveals itself when, having dwelled in His presence, loved your neighbor as yourself, and practiced "I am He," you have ripened in His peace. The way home is through His peace to love.

A RESTLESS MIND

Q: One of the obstacles to inner calm is when the mind refuses to let go and it prevails over inner peace.

A: You talk of peace as if it were just a kind of stillness, but what are you really dealing with here?

Q: With God in the form of "I Am." With Mā.

A: So, what do you want to improve about Mā?

Q: I don't want to improve anything, but my mental agitation is often more powerful than Mā and takes up more space!

A: The state you describe is when your mind is churning, when you cannot find peace and you are under the impression that your restless thoughts are you, instead of having the dignity of being Mā. Who is being manifested in the form of these thoughts? Do you have a personal thought factory inside your head? Do you create your thoughts?

Q: No!

A: Who sustains the existence of thoughts?

Q: Mā does.

A: And where are you when you realize that your thoughts are also Hers?

Q: I can sometimes stand back but I often get carried away by them.

A: You let yourself be carried away because you believe that you are your thoughts and you allow yourself be affected by them. Let's look once again at how this mechanism works: who sustains thoughts?

Q: Mā.

A: When you realize this, where are you?

Q: Either I realize that everything belongs to Mā or I realize that I too belong to Mā.

A: Exactly! There you have it. Be in communion with Mā. And then, are there any thoughts? Remain in communion with "I Am," for whom thoughts are mere ripples. If you have a toddler one day and it begins to cry, are you going to smack it to calm it down? Thoughts are like crying toddlers, running all over the place doing what comes to them naturally. Be like a mother to them and do what mothers do. Be Mā, whether in Her peace or in the absence of Her peace. When you live with the dignity of being "I Am," you will begin to experience deep calm.

Thoughts are also connected to actions and you cannot experience inner calm if you act from an egoic territory. Egoic territories take time to dissolve, and because the aim here is not to defend the egoic territory, always be ready to question your actions. Look at them in the light of God's presence, and His peace, which is the essence of your interiority, will guide you on the path of wisdom and goodness.

BEING REAL

When people are on the path of spiritual awakening, they often think that they have to change or improve their present state, or alter it to conform to some previous experience. For example, many people meditate in the hopes of no longer being tormented by their thoughts.

Why not just be your natural, uncontrived self? Let your present state be as it is; don't try to make something out of it. The natural state of your being is an expression of what Is, an expression of That which Is, a vast, never-ending ocean of love. It may not be revealed, granted, so what? "Being That" is your birthright and your highest duty in life. Be That by the strength of your belief in the words of Christ, "I and my Father are one," a belief that enables us to bear witness on earth to the love of the divine Father. Grounded in this belief, your actions will unfold according to the light of the Spirit, a beacon that guides us to perfection. And with that, be happy!

BEYOND DUALITY: THE STEADFASTNESS OF BEING

Q: Why is it that one day I can feel full of light and the next day, for no apparent reason, I'm overcome by black misery that I find difficult to shake off? I find it hard to deal with.

A: The light you speak of is just a mental idea you have of God. Life manifests in many different ways and you must have absolute faith in whatever form it manifests in, because, in reality, it is in God that you are putting your faith.

He is there in the form of presence? Fine. He is there in the form of absence? That's fine too. Let yourself be carried by life, because its sole purpose is to reveal to you gradually that you are the divine Being, who is aware of both presence and absence; that is to say, the unchanging part of you where you are one with the Infinite. The quality of spiritual life is not measured by "light" or physical well-being, but by the steadfastness of your faith in God when you are faced with the challenges and difficulties of life.

FIRST LET YOURSELF BE FILLED BY PEACE

Q: Yesterday during meditation when you suggested we visualize Swami Chidananda, I felt very close to him and a great peace came over me. I asked myself, "Who sees this?" Then I felt something expand inside me, if I can put like that—it's hard to put into words what I felt—but as soon as I started looking at what was happening, the feeling disappeared. I said to myself, "I must let go of the mind," and as soon as I gave up any mental effort, I felt I could go deeper and deeper. What should we make of this sort of experience?

A: Excellent! Your experience is that of an ocean wave coming into deep communion with water. Beneath the wave is the ocean that you are. You felt a great peace, and the question "Who sees this?" that you so rightly asked yourself awakened a flash of the Spirit, an experience that you describe as an expansion.

43

If you try to grasp That which sees, it will elude you, because a wave cannot grasp the ocean. The Spirit that you are cannot be attained, it can only be revealed through faith. It arises in your life like the morning sun that rises gradually in the sky to reach its midday zenith.

This kind of experience shows you the direction in which the Spirit in you lies, and is there to encourage you on the path.

CONCEPTS ARE BORN AND DIE: REALITY REMAINS

Q: How do you anchor yourself in reality?

A: How can you be anything other than anchored in reality? Isn't reality always present? Our problem is that we create an unreality that masks plain, simple reality. When you say, "I am my nationality," "I am my job," "I am my political opinions," "I am my age," you superimpose a mountain of ideas on a simple, everlasting reality, on existence itself. Your mistake is that you invest your love and belief in impermanent concepts and live disconnected from reality, which alone is unchanging.

This is illustrated by the following story. Once upon a time there was a field with shepherds and shepherdesses. A wide street was built down the middle of the field, which was lavishly lit and decorated. It was named the Champs Elysées, the "Elysian Fields." As people wanted to enjoy themselves, they opened a music hall nearby and called it the Folies Bergères, "The Follies of the Shepherdesses." This proved a huge success, so they built a cabaret with a windmill on top and called it Le Moulin Rouge, "The Red Windmill," after the mills that used to operate in the area. Then a Mr. Eiffel came along and constructed an iron tower, like a child playing with Legos. More buildings went up on either side of the Champs Elysées and foreigners came to enjoy themselves. "What fun it is here," they said, "it's Paris!" And now you only have to say the word "Paris" for everyone to think of the Champs Elysées, the Folies Bergères, and the Eiffel Tower!

Which is more real, the field that was there thousands of years ago—and will no doubt be there again thousands of years hence—or the names and forms that have been superimposed on the field? We unconsciously endow our creations with a quality of truth and eternity. But the only reality, the

44

only eternal factor, is the interiority we experience as our soul, and it is by living connected to this that we fulfill our true purpose in life.

When a drop of water falls onto a lake, it "creates" ripples on the surface of the water. But has anything actually been created? The ripples add nothing new, they do not cancel out the water, nor do they coexist with it: they are simply a modification of it.

The ripples on the surface of the water "Paris" are nothing but mental constructs that prevent you from being aware of the reality "water" and "field." Is there life in the concept "Paris"? No, and yet you believe in it! Of course, you have to use concepts, but the world of concepts should not take up your entire existence, as if the external world were the only truth. Whoever lives like this is dead to life.

Q: My question is linked to another: how can I distinguish between God's will and my own desires?

A: Do you belong to the idea you have of yourself or do you belong to life? If you belong to the idea you have of yourself, then there might be a god who says to each person individually "do this" or "do that." But if the will of this god was constantly in conflict with your own desires, how long do you think you could put up with being dictated to by an outside force, even if it was coming from a god? Your true body is the body of life, the body of "I Am," and not the idea you have of yourself. Life is a current and that current is God's will. It is the tangible expression of the Infinite that reveals to you, in the here and now, where you are one with Him.

You are not here to act so much as to let yourself be acted upon. You are not here to carry a burden, but to let yourself be carried by your inner life. You are not here to live in fear, but to live with trust in His presence. You are not here to judge, but to realize that the whole world is His expression. You are not here to believe in a God that is separate from you, but to believe in your dignity of being one with Him.

IT ISN'T THAT COMPLICATED

Q: One day on a retreat you asked us to visualize the Virgin Mary, or any other holy figure, and imagine that she was holding us in her arms. I found this a very powerful image but it also bothered me. I was drawn to it because it helped me let go, but at the same time I didn't know what position I should be in, whether I should let myself be held by the Virgin or whether I should put my arms around her neck. I tried to practice after the retreat but gave up in the end because it was too complicated.

A: We tend to complicate what is very simple. The instructions I gave for the meditation were as follows: imagine yourself in the presence of the Holy Virgin and lay your head on her lap, just as you laid your head on your mother's lap when you were a child. Begin by feeling her presence, and don't complicate things with the details of your position! Was it so difficult to put your head on your mother's knee and feel comfortable? Stop struggling with your mind and let the meditation unfold.

I also told you to be "as if" in deep sleep—a key aspect of the meditation that you left out. In life we experience three states: waking, dreaming, and deep sleep. In deep sleep the intellect is absorbed by the state, there is nothing; the world is neither present nor absent, and yet you are there. You are all experts in this state as you have experienced it nearly every night since you were born.

The technique that consists in resting on the knees of the divine Mother "as if" in deep sleep prevents the mind's old habit of disturbing your inner space with its attempts to measure, analyze, and grasp the truth. It allows you to drink the nectar of immortality of His peace. Persevere in the practice and you will succeed. But don't forget that you should think you are in a state of deep sleep and not actually fall asleep! Under no circumstances should you lose consciousness.

BECOMING POOR LIKE A CHILD

Q: How can I increase the strength of the divine breath in me in order to free myself from the conditioning that shapes my life?

A: By becoming poor again, like a child.

Q: It'll take so long!

A: That depends on the strength of your desire to realize God. The state of being like a child is here for you now, immediately. Children are straightforward and poor in attributes—they are not this or that, they just are. When you remain in this childlike state, you become aware of a great depth. And if, with faith no larger than a mustard seed, you bring a sense of sacredness to this depth, it then includes everyone and everything, even the furthest stars, time, space, the entire universe. Until now, you have been using your intellect to help you reach this depth, but once you realize that the stillness there is sacred, you can give up the old mental struggle and, as it were, rest your head on the pillow of sacredness. Use a personal concept of God if you wish. You then discover an even deeper, inexpressible state called *ishvara,* which is the state of deep sleep in the waking state. In this state, search for the "I" that sees the state. You can use the *neti-neti* technique,[2] for example. Where "I" is revealed is He that is unknowable, ineffable, adorable. He that no meditation can reach. He that not even the word "God" can describe. The only term you can use to express what is revealed is "Spirit." You are That. All you need then do is be, and grow in goodness so that your actions bear witness to the divine love that you are.

Live with the conviction "I and my Father are one," or proclaim like Shankaracharya, the great sage of Advaita, *"chidananda rupa shivoham shivoham,"* "I am Shiva, in the form of absolute consciousness, bliss"; it is the most powerful form of the divine breath "I Am." Be like a roaring lion and inwardly assert the dignity of being the immortal, divine Self, and not some feeble creature moaning about the indignities of life. Then the full force of His peace will flow to the Infinite that you are.

Don't try to manipulate your inner state; let it be as it is and know that the Almighty is present. Rest there. Be patient with yourself. An apple does not ripen in a day, and it takes determination and perseverance to dissolve the egoic territory. The whole universe is but a ripple of His Peace. Don't let yourself be impressed by the world of human beings and their dreams; do what you have to do without getting caught up in other people's dreams. Life is a current that flows in two directions: toward God or toward the cosmic dream. You cannot follow both.

IT'S IMPOSSIBLE TO MEDITATE!

Q: I find it difficult to meditate.

A: The problem arises because you have not yet made God the purpose of your life. Meditation is not the result of practicing at a particular time of the day; when you have decided that you want God and God alone, now, in this lifetime, it is there with your every breath.

Q: But I have faith.

A: Yes, but have you made God the purpose of your life to the exclusion of everything else? If your life were dedicated to Him, difficulties in meditation would not arise. The pages of your life are already written, down to the last comma, and the dream images are there to reveal to you the divine light that you are. Meditate deeply on the following truth: what you should have, you will be given; what you should not have, you will not be given. By making God the purpose of your life, you awaken to the truth; you fulfill your duty as a human being and discover the glory of your divinity. Stop worrying and abide in His peace.

MAKING GOD YOUR BEST FRIEND

Q: You've told us to make God our best friend. Could you explain what you mean by that?

A: Under certain conditions, everyone you consider a friend in the world can voluntarily or involuntarily let you down. During the tsunami in Indonesia, for example, a mother and child were swept away in the water. The mother tried desperately to hold on to her child, but the water was oily and in spite of all her efforts the child slipped from her arms. A child trusts its mother, who is often ready to give up her life for her child, and yet in this instance the child may have felt abandoned or betrayed. In fact, when you put your trust in the world, the world will one day forsake you.

God is the only friend fully worthy of your trust. Put your life in his hands and trust in him with all your heart.

THE LORD'S PRAYER

Q: I like the Lord's Prayer very much. Can I use it as a mantra? Could you explain its meaning?

A: Reciting the rosary with the Lord's Prayer is exactly the same as repeating a mantra. But don't forget that is just as important to believe in His presence and to feel peace and silence, because He is that peace.

The prayer begins "Our Father who art in heaven." The word "heaven" represents the Absolute, an ocean of bliss.

"Hallowed be thy name." God and His name are one. Repetition of His name is the surest, quickest, and most effective way of ripening in His peace.

"Thy kingdom come." What governs your interiority? Make it His peace in all circumstances, in joy and sorrow, in success and failure, in sickness and health, in life and in death.

"Thy will be done, on earth as it is in heaven." What is God's will? It is not a commandment given by some God on high to you as a person, as if God were outside you. God's will is that you live aligned with the current that flows to the Infinite. Everyone has a sense of existence, of "I Am," and this requires no effort of will. But effort and will are required in order to become aware of peace and silence, and this is what God wants. The Supreme Being is an ocean of love that wants only what is best for you: that you return to where you are one with Him. Jesus said, "The kingdom of heaven is within." By connecting to His peace, you live in harmony with the kingdom of heaven. Your actions here on earth must also reflect the nature of His peace, which is an ocean of infinite goodness and wisdom.

"Give us this day our daily bread." "Daily bread" refers not only to the bread you eat and which your body requires, but to another kind of need that has to be satisfied in order for you to ripen in His peace. A retreat provides this kind of nourishment, one that is necessary for awakening. Reading the scriptures, keeping the company of people who are also on the spiritual path, visiting holy sites, and celebrating religious festivals are other forms of nourishment.

"Forgive us our trespasses, as we forgive them that trespass against us." Imperfection is inevitable in this world. We all make mistakes from time to time, and it is only to be expected that people should wrong us; you should not dwell on it.

"Lead us not into temptation, but deliver us from evil." The current of life that flows toward the external world is called desire, which creates an egoic territory that blinds us to the suffering we can cause in pursuit of our satisfaction. Only faith in the presence of God can free us from the grip of the egoic territory.

SOUNDS AND SILENCE

Q: I sometimes find it difficult to say my prayers and mantras, because although I feel a strong pull in that direction I also find all those words disturbing, even though they are spiritual. I'm scared of saying them because what you're talking about frightens me. I feel that if I say the words, I'll fall into something vast. This both attracts and terrifies me, because it's unknown.

A: What you describe is a wave frightened of its own "water-ness," a wave that senses the profound depths into which it could disappear. It is the idea you have of being a person that feels fear when confronted with inner reality. This is why the scriptures clearly state that dwelling in *saguna brahman*, God in a concrete, personal form, is an essential stage before abiding in *nirguna brahman*, "I Am," or God in an abstract form. In order to get rid of the false, but concrete, idea you have of yourself, you need a concrete concept of God. If, for example, you take the concept of the Immaculate Conception and apply it to your sense of inner peace, that peace will feel increasingly less frightening until you reach the point when it is no longer frightening at all. You are simply able to abide in Her peace, however profound, and feel comfortable, because you have placed your faith in Her. Inner peace is identical to the state of the world before creation, just as water is the state of the ocean before the creation of waves.

Q: You've said that silence is important, but don't sounds or thoughts obscure silence to a certain extent?

A: Once again, your problem is that you think you are a separate person. You believe that you are the one who is doing, acting, speaking, and so on. You think that thoughts and words cut you off from the Infinite, and this makes you feel guilty. The problem will be resolved when you no longer feel that it is you who speaks, acts, or thinks, but when you firmly believe that it is life that is doing it. Life does everything and life contains everything. All words and thoughts are contained in life; when you realize this, you can use all the words you like, it will no longer be important. In this way, you ripen in His peace without losing your human dimension, because the Infinite includes the finite, just as the ocean includes the waves. And when you have ripened, you will no longer need an idea of God, such as the Immaculate Conception, but until that point. . . .

As far as the relationship between sounds and silence is concerned, there are three possibilities: first, that sounds cancel out silence; second, that sounds and silence coexist—silence being perhaps the foundation of sounds; the third possibility, the correct one, is that sound is nothing other than a modification of silence. When you use the concept of the Immaculate Conception, for example, the sound/silence question resolves itself automatically, because there the two are one. Whatever your thoughts, and however powerful the resulting drive that compels you to seek happiness in the external world, everything you could ever want is in the here and now of "I Am," even the furthest stars. When you live with that conviction, true joy and true happiness arise and you gradually find it easier to remain in silence because you are in the company of God.

THE CURE FOR FEAR

Q: Is there a cure for fear?

A: The cure for fear is to practice the presence of God. At this very moment you feel nothing. But if you shut your eyes and recite a prayer, while being very aware of the presence of God, there is peace. A minute ago, you felt nothing and now His peace is there. What made the difference? The presence of God.

This presence leads to interiority, which you experience and interpret as fear because the concept you have of yourself is still deeply ingrained and has crystallized, a bit like water in an ice cube. In order for fear to disappear, you have to wait for the concept to dissolve, and for this to happen you have to let yourself be filled by His presence.

Fear will never give you any respite until you live in harmony with His will, which is present here in the form of peace. This is the measure of whether your spiritual life is going in the right direction.

The divine Spirit that you are is absolutely free from fear. Fear is nothing but the pull of the Infinite calling you home. When you answer the call, fear gradually goes out of your life forever.

THE CARAPACE

Q: In order to be able maintain a state of inner stillness, I've built up a carapace, a hard shell around myself. Should I let it dissolve or should I preserve it so as to remain in peace?

A: Both. If you are sheltering behind this carapace and it has become "your" shell, it must dissolve. Find out what concept you are clinging to—it is the root cause of your egoic territory—and expose it to the presence of God. If, for example, you lose your temper easily, the source of your anger might be "my" opinion, "my" country, or "my" religion. The possibilities are endless. But if you observe your reactions in the light of the presence of God, you learn how to act from divine Consciousness and not from the carapace of an egoic territory. It is then up to you to find the courage to do what is right.

If, however, the shell you describe is the cave of your heart, where you practice loving God in the form of peace, then it is where your spiritual practice takes place and it is a sacred place, which includes everyone and everything. It is where you love God in the form of inner peace and you practice believing that everything is here, in His hands, in His peace. The aim is not to remain cocooned in your own little world, but to bring this sacred place into all your actions in a simple, straightforward way. Life does everything, from the blossoming of a flower to the birth of a star; everything happens within His peace. Seen in this way, the world becomes a mirror that reflects the Spirit that you are.

DO WHATEVER YOU ENJOY

Q: Some people find peace in music, in playing the guitar, for example; others find it in drawing, painting or climbing mountains. So doesn't the path to peace depend on the activities we choose to do?

A: No, but they are not incompatible. It is important that whatever activity you take up should bring you peace. Playing the guitar or the piano, painting, sailing, walking in the mountains—all these can help you feel the peace and presence of God, and can therefore help you abide in interiority. One day you will no longer need these props because His peace will completely fill you. Until then, do whatever you enjoy. When you enjoy something it opens you, and when you are open there is peace. That peace is God. Realize this truth.

Q: But you have to be sure to make the right choices on the path to peace?

A: When you decide that it is time to awaken and you make God the purpose of your life, the right choices will make themselves spontaneously. If, on a human level, you have the opportunity to do the things you enjoy, so much the better. But life does not always turn out the way we want it. Sometimes you find yourself in situations where you have to do things you do not enjoy, and you have to accept those too. You don't impose conditions on the Absolute!

FINDING A PARTNER AT SIXTY

Q: Is finding a partner and forming a relationship at sixty incompatible with undertaking sadhana?

A: Many sages in India were married until the day they died, so being in a relationship is not incompatible with sadhana and awakening to the Spirit. But there is a time for everything. At sixty, your health begins to decline; you have less energy, and any energy you expend looking for a new partner will not be there for your search for God. Life's precious gift of time is flying by and you are not on this earth forever. So ask yourself what you really want: God or a companion? It is up to you.

Q: What about the tender, loving aspect of a relationship, the caring and sharing?

A: The idea that you need a companion is due to uncontrolled desires, to a lack of mental discipline. "Seek ye first the Kingdom of God and His righteousness, and all these things shall be added unto you."[3] If you really want God above all else, don't you think that He knows exactly what you need and will provide it? But if it is you who decides "This is what I need," you create an egoic territory. Which are you going to trust, your desires or He that knows?

It is useful to look at the teachings of the sages on the subject. Ideally, according to Indian tradition, life is divided into four periods of twenty-five years. The first is for education, to ensure success in life, and should focus exclusively on study; love relationships are excluded.

During the second stage it is time to marry, raise a family, and work, making room all the while for God. This is the period when you ripen in His peace until it fills your being, and then, like St. Paul, you can say, "I live; yet not I, but Christ liveth in me."

The third stage is one of prerenunciation, when you remain constantly in "I Am" and awaken to the Spirit.

The fourth stage is renunciation: you have realized the divine Spirit, you are anchored in the Infinite, and you bear witness to the immeasurable love that fills your being.

Loneliness, depression, and boredom are messengers that recur in your life to call you back to the Infinite, to your glorious origin whose nature is absolute bliss. What will you do at ninety, when it is too late to find a companion to help you sweep unhappiness under the carpet? It will be too late then to awaken. Once again, you will have missed the opportunity and regrets will be useless at that stage.

Reflect on what have you done with your life so far. Where do you want to be at the moment of death? Life is a precious gift. The best use to which you can put it is to find the Spirit, where you are one with the Infinite, where you are free and bliss is absolute. If this is what you want above all else, it is revealed to you. This is an infallible law and an irrefutable truth.

Reality or dream? There comes a time when you have to decide; you cannot follow both directions at once.

CHANNELING, ANGELS, AND CO.

Q: What are your views on channeling, communicating with angels, and so on?

A: They are ways of trying to sweep the intolerable burden of inner silence under the carpet, of avoiding the simple practice of remaining in the presence of God in the form of inner stillness. The concept you have of being the body and mind, the "I-thought," cannot tolerate the idea of abiding in stillness; nor can it accept the practice recommended by sages of renouncing the idea "I am the body" and of identifying with the body of His peace, of acknowledging God and seeking fulfillment in Him. This implies hard work, a period of solitude, and a time in the wilderness. And, until this identification becomes natural, it requires single-mindedness, a change of perspective, and an effort of faith.

Rather than encouraging you along this path, some people try to distract you by playing with the forces of the dream world. Because of the many different forms of its forces, the cosmic universe, which is an expression of "I Am," becomes the playground of the ignorant, too impatient to await the moment of awakening. This is where you will find a whole array of people channeling the dead, communicating with "beings of light" or trying to heal by transmitting "God's energy". You will also find so-called masters with half-baked ideas "initiating" those who, like children craving a new toy, are prepared to try anything rather than face inner stillness.

The Infinite never communicates with the concept you have of yourself, but only through "I Am," when His grace touches you by means of a dream, a vision, or a spiritual experience. These are to guide and encourage you on your spiritual journey. They never occur on your terms, so they can never come about through "channeling."

Q: After reading Gitta Mallasz's *Dialogues with the Angel* I had a very powerful experience that woke me in the middle of the night with this question: "What is faith?" It wasn't a word in my vocabulary at the time and I know it was connected to the book. The experience set me on the path, but after what you've just said, I wonder whether my experience was authentic. Does it mean that you can't have an authentic experience from a book of this kind?

A: At the time you were not interested in God, but the book opened you to His presence. It was your gateway to the spiritual path. That is excellent, and many other people have also no doubt benefited in the same way. Fine. But that does not necessarily stamp the book with a certificate of authenticity as a guide on the path to the Infinite.

You are the light of the Spirit. Contemplate God in whatever form you choose: in the clouds, sky, sea, or mountains; in the wind, stars, sun, cosmos, or beauties of nature. But if you really want to know yourself and return to the house of the divine Father, you must pass through the love of God in the form of "I Am"; through the love of God in the simple prayer of communion with interiority. If someone gives a teaching that means taking advice from a being up above, even an angel, let me tell you right away that I am not interested in that kind of communication! The God that you experience directly in the form of inner stillness is infinitely superior to any angel that communicates through the intermediary of another person.

What did Christ say? "I am the way, the truth, and the life: no man cometh unto the Father, but by me." Interiority is the only path that leads to knowledge. This implies investing your belief in the fact that interiority is God and that it includes everything and everyone. It presupposes a certain effort and excludes petty distractions. In reality, these distractions deny the fact of God: you either have God or you have angels; you cannot have both.

If you choose angels, then you are going to be distracted from turning within and you will avoid the necessary confrontation with peace, silence, and solitude. The steps on the road to Self-knowledge are as follows: first, "Love the Lord thy God with all thine heart, and with all thy soul, and with all thy might"[4]—that is to say, love "I Am," the stillness of interiority, because it is God in tangible form. Secondly, "Love thy neighbor as thyself": see that everyone and everything is part of interiority. A pebble, a blade of grass, a tree, a bird, and the stars all share in the life that is in you in the form of peace and silence. They are all here in Him. This is the path that leads you home to the Infinite.

In India, the path is contained in the prayer *"asato ma sad gamaya,"* "lead me from the unreal to the real." The unreal is exteriority, with all its names, forms, and distractions. The real is what lies within interiority.

If you want to play in the external world with Brahma, the creator, He is quite happy to play with you. But then you remain in the dream, a bit like children at nursery school who spend all day playing. To seek distractions in the world is to remain at a nursery-school level. It all depends on what you want. Many people want a house, wealth, or power—the distractions the world has to offer are endless—and there are others who seek spiritual distractions. The ignorance is the same in both cases. These people have lost sight of the fact that the precious gift of human life has one purpose and one purpose only: to return to the house of the Father.

3.

DIFFICULTIES ON THE PATH

KNOWING, LOVING, AND BELIEVING

Q: My difficulty is that in order to reach a state of inner peace, I use my mind, and then it's hard to let go of it.

A: Yes, you're right. When you focus your thoughts on a single object, the mind reaches a certain depth of stillness where it can experience various states of samadhi. These experiences are obtained through the intellect.

But there is more at work here: there are the acts of knowing, loving, and believing, which, unlike the stillness of interiority, can never become objects of experience. They cannot be grasped because they are in the here and now, between two images, between two thoughts, transcending time and space. It is there that you discover the Spirit that you are.

The power of knowing, "chit" in Sanskrit, is what knows, for example, that at midday it is daytime. Let me give you a clearer idea of what I mean. Take a three-month-old baby, an age at which the intellect is not yet developed and cannot therefore interfere. The baby's state is Spirit, but it has not yet awakened to its Being. The nature of Spirit is awareness and if you observe the baby you will see that it is a bundle of awareness. You will also notice that a three-month-old baby loves everyone indiscriminately. It is not that *it* loves a person: it is the Spirit, love itself, that loves. But you, who are the light of the world, suffer because you have forgotten that your true nature is plenitude. The love that you are seeks fulfillment in the world of name and form. You, who are love, invest your love poorly. All actions spring from love: even a robber who holds up a bank and kills an employee is acting from love, a love invested in the idea that money will bring him happiness.

The power of knowing and loving is characterized by a third faculty, that of believing, or faith. In the morning, when you look at the sun, you are sure it is rising. When you look at it at night, you are sure it is setting. But is it really so? Of course not. And yet everyone believes it! That is what I call faith. Nonbelievers say, "I don't believe in God," but with what do they believe their disbelief? With the power of belief applied to disbelief. It is impossible not to believe, because faith is not a human quality; it is not something you "have," it is what you are. At this very moment, you believe you are in such-and-such a place, in such-and-such a town, in such-and-such a country. The entire mountain of concepts that make up human life are based on the power of belief.

The power of knowing, loving, and believing is the light that you are. Jesus said, "Ye are the light of the world."[1] The question is to know how you are going to invest this power. In India, we recite the prayer *"asatoma ma sad gamaya"*: "lead me from the unreal to the real." The unreal is the world of concepts in which we live. Our idea of New York, for example, is nothing but a mental concept. What is real is interiority. The billions of known and unknown universes are of no significance whatsoever compared to inner peace, because that peace is God. We need to have faith in order to move from the concept we have of ourselves and our surroundings to interiority. This does not mean that we become unintelligent or incapable of action; on the contrary. The path to awakening is through faith.

REJECTING GOD

The more room you make in your life for peace, for life, the greater your capacity to see and listen to other people from within interiority, from within that sacred space where people are seen not as outside you, but are recognized as belonging to the life within you. Then nothing in the world, whatever it may be, is separate from that space.

But can you do this if you have not first acknowledged the divine in your interiority? Can you achieve it if you substitute a mental concept for the divine?

This morning someone told me that they saw peace as a great vastness, but does this vastness include other people? Does the idea of vastness include that sacred and adorable reality that manifests in the form of this cosmic universe? With the power of thought, you can conjure up any idea or dream, but if you want to include everyone in interiority and awaken to divine love, the one and only path is to love God in the form of "I Am."

I know that many of you are allergic to the word "God," which has been dragged through the mud by human error and egoic territories that are responsible for unspeakable acts. Most wars have been fought in the name of God. It seems incredible that a king of France, who ruled over a peaceful and prosperous kingdom, could set off on a Crusade having had a religious experience that he interpreted as a message from God. "Go and deliver the Holy Land," it said! Convinced that God was on his side, the king went into battle, sacrificed thousands of men, wounded many others, and brought ruin on his kingdom.

The staunchly Christian kings of Spain conquered South America and massacred the Native people there instead of heeding the message of Christ and acknowledging them as brothers. There is no shortage of examples of ways in which the Church has acted as a political organization, greedy for power and money. Hence the message Christ gave to St. Francis of Assisi, in the small church of St. Damian where the saint had retired to pray, "Francis, go and repair my house, which you see is falling down." Initially, St. Francis thought this meant repair the building itself, which was badly dilapidated. It was several years before he realized that Christ's message referred to the Church and its ways.

Some years ago I was in Paris with my master, Swami Chidananda, at the house of one of his disciples, a Lebanese Christian. The news on television had angered our host: A community of Polish Carmelite nuns had established a convent at Auschwitz and the Jewish community was violently opposing it. Fierce discussions were taking place between Jewish and Christian authorities and neither side would budge from its position. As a Christian, my fellow disciple could not sanction the Jewish community's attitude and turned to Swami Chidananda to seek his opinion. I was glad to be present and curious to know what Swamiji's position would be, given that there was, after all, right on both sides.

Swami Chidananda simply answered: "Doesn't Jesus say, 'If your brother is angry with you, then leave your prayers and first be reconciled with him'?[2] He doesn't say 'If you are angry with him,' but 'if he is angry with you.'"

The message of Christ is not easy to put into practice, because it is not based on human reasoning but on interiority, which includes everyone. Interiority is like a reed that bends in the wind and adapts to circumstances, while the egoic territory is like an oak that stands its ground and refuses to bow.

My spiritual brother and I were astonished by the simplicity and wisdom of Swamiji's reply. When you love God in the form of "I Am," you have no need to refer to the scriptures, because it is "I Am," in the form of your true Self, that acts and speaks with wisdom. If, on the other hand, you try to say and do "the right thing" while remaining identified with your humanity, wise actions and words will always elude you.

For all sorts of reasons, many of you have grown up rejecting the word "God" completely: "If that's your God and if that's what has been done in his name, then I'm not interested in your God!" But the God that has led to so many barbarous acts is a mind-made God and is not real. If you look closely, you will see that the reasons you reject God are related to human problems and errors, not to God.

The world we live in is a result of how we invest our light. You can love God in the form of inner peace and become like St. Francis, or you can live a life of frustration and blame God and the rest of the world for your problems. You are the light of the world and you create the world you live in. By rejecting God, you ignore a universal reality, an interiority that includes everyone and everything. When you invest your faith in interiority, it awakens you to the divine Spirit and the word "God" falls away as inadequate. It is then that you are reconciled with God, with the world, and with yourself.

TRUSTING IN GOD

Q: You said that God never lets you down. But I went through a very painful experience, and although I put my trust in God, and in spite of all my hard work and devotion, he let me down and went out of my life. I felt betrayed. This happened about ten years ago and it changed everything. I'm coming back to him little by little, but I say to myself, "He's been out of my life for so long, do I really need him?"

A: I understand. I am glad you brought up the subject, because it is often a source of misunderstanding. "God never betrays you" does not mean that everything always happens on your own terms. The purpose of life is to reveal to you the Infinite that you are. The God you speak of is a God in your mind, God as a thought-form; it is not God. People who go to church, to a synagogue or mosque, often put their whole faith in the God of their church, synagogue, or mosque.

The basis of all religion is prayer, the purpose of which is to ripen you to interiority, where God is real and tangible. Some years ago in America, an explosion trapped a group of miners at the bottom of a mine. Their families went to church to pray. Someone came and told them that all the miners were safe and well, it seemed, except for one man. Everyone rejoiced. "We prayed to God and He has answered our prayers! Thank you, Jesus! God was really with us!" Then terrible news followed: "Sorry, there has been a mix-up. In fact, all but one of the men are dead." The families, religious believers all, were faced with a choice: either they put their faith in God and in life as it had manifested, or they rejected Him and lived in anger and doubt. People often choose the second option.

The role of life is to curb the egoic territory and reveal to you where you are one with the Eternal. If you live connected to God through interiority, you can face even the most difficult challenges in life. There is sometimes a heavy price to pay, but it cannot compare with the bliss that is then yours.

You are always right to put your trust in God. When you answer the call of the Infinite, suffering no longer has a role to play; its job is done and it goes out of your life forever.

ABORTION

Q: I find myself in a difficult situation and I'm frightened of God's anger. I've just found out that I'm pregnant. It was an accident and my boyfriend and I don't think it's the right time to start a family. We've only known each other for two months and it seems too soon. As he hasn't met you yet, it's difficult for me to talk to him about God's will. Could the fact that it doesn't seem to be the right time be a manifestation of God's will? Since He is All, I say to myself that if we decide on an abortion, then it's His will, but I'm not sure. Please can you help me?

A: I understand your situation. It is not a question of fearing God's anger, but of the effect an abortion will have on your life. You are the one carrying the child, not your boyfriend. It is not a joint pregnancy, nor would it be a joint abortion. A child is a great responsibility, but one that brings great joy and love into your life. A child does not belong to you or to your boyfriend; it has a life of its own. If you have an abortion, you will be damaging something in you that will be very difficult to repair. If you have another child, you will always remember this one with sorrow. The women I have met on my retreats who have had abortions bitterly regret it.

A child forces you to sort out your priorities. Keep it, and inwardly make God the purpose of your life. Life will look after you both, even if your boyfriend does not want you to keep it. Don't be afraid! Don't be afraid! Om!

THE ROLE OF SUFFERING

Q: How is it possible not to be angry with God when you see all the wars and suffering going on around us, and for the simple reason that he has created such an imperfect world?

A: The God you are talking about is a God in your mind, a God you think about. You think about the Immortal with a mortal brain, about the Infinite with a finite intellect, about That which has never taken birth with a mind that has been born: the God of your thoughts is a poor God. It is not God!

One day an elderly man, a regular churchgoer, lost his wife. In his unhappiness he rejected God, blaming him for letting his wife die. Why did the man react in this way when he had been to church every Sunday of his life? Because the God he believed in was a God in his mind. He had not ripened in the stillness of interiority. That is where prayer is real and that is where you must direct your thoughts, until such a time as concentration, which inevitably requires effort in the beginning, becomes natural.

The world appears to be a chaotic expression of the Infinite and, from a relative point of view, seems imperfect. It is, in fact, absolutely perfect, the perfect expression of truth. Suffering is the mechanism that forces us to turn toward God; it is the expression of an everlasting love that drives us toward Him with incredible force and wants only for us to return to the bliss of the Infinite. The good and bad things that happen to us are the consequence of our actions, and these in turn are the direct result of what we believe and love. It is convenient to look only at the people who suffer, and to forget those whose actions are the cause of suffering. What happens to the people who inflict suffering? They will undergo, in full measure, the exact consequences of their actions. After death, they will wait in limbo for thousands of years before obtaining another human birth, and then only to experience an identical suffering to the one they inflicted. That is what hell is! The laws of nature are perfect and implacable: all action creates an equal and opposite reaction and, whether you believe it or not, these laws apply to everyone.

But as soon as you decide to return to the divine Father and abide in His peace, which is the opportunity afforded to you by this human life, your actions become right actions as a matter of course. When you answer the call of the Infinite, your sins are forgiven, and if your karma is to have your head cut off, only your hat will be snatched away instead. Fear and suffering gradually leave your life, never to return.

Q: Why do we have to go through all this suffering just to go back to what we already are?

A: When you are at the cinema, the movie lasts for a couple of hours. In the movie, space, time, and causality, with its rules of good and evil, operate. It seems, for example, to be thanks to John Wayne that the baddie gets killed. But once the movie is over and you go into the projection room, you can look at the filmstrip and see all the frames at once. There is no chain of cause and effect between one image and the next, and time was just a consequence of the light being projected onto moving images.

Have you noticed the similarities in people's descriptions of near-death experience? They see their whole life flash by in an instant. Each image is seen clearly, not in the space of two or three minutes, not even in the space of ten seconds, but in the immediacy of the present moment. Some people report that they even relived the emotions associated with events, both theirs and the ones they had caused. Often during this experience a divine being asks them what they have done with their life.

These experiences, which are not uncommon, are important because they reveal information about the nature of the world and of life here on earth. The most significant piece of information is that the divine being says, "Well, you were given a spiritual Ferrari, that is to say a human life, and what have you done with it?"

And you, oh, light of the Spirit, who, thanks to this human body, can experience life as if you held it in the palm of your hand, you who have the possibility of making room in your life for Life and awakening to the Spirit, what have you done with your life?

Near-death experiences are also important because they show that the world, exactly as in a movie, is made up of a sequence of unfolding images, names, and forms. It is you, the light of the world, who, because you invest your belief and love in the world of name and form, sustains the dream world and generates the storyline of lives to come.

Everyone lives in the bubble of their own dream, but if you want to awaken to the truth of your Being you must connect with the very source of the dream, with interiority, which includes everyone and everything. When you connect to life, it is gradually revealed to you that you are That or, in the words of Jesus, "the Father." Then you no longer need to seek fulfillment in future births; you are enlightened and free. To enlightened beings there is a paradox: past, present, and future merge into the here and now, and they realize that all their lives and births had no more substance than a dream.

Q: But the vast majority of people aren't interested in all this and yet, in spite of everything, most people manage to do good in their lives. Aren't they doing the right thing?

A: The Upanishads state that whoever does what is right, or whoever does their duty, spontaneously realizes the divine Self and is liberated in this lifetime. But is it always so easy to do your duty? At every step there is a corresponding right action. To be happy and make those around you happy is one way of doing the right thing, but do most people succeed? If you want to be happy in every circumstance, you must learn not so much to live as "to be lived."

"YE OF LITTLE FAITH"

Q: In the episode where the disciples are on a boat with Jesus and a storm starts up, Jesus says, "O ye of little faith."[3] Was this because if the disciples had had faith, they too could have calmed the storm?

A: What do you think?

Q: Perhaps at that moment they weren't ready. It was only after the Resurrection that they would have had the power.

A: Then why would Jesus have said "Ye of little faith"?

Q: Because they didn't believe in him; they didn't believe that when they were with him nothing could happen to them.

A: Is Jesus God?

Q: For me, yes.

A: So the disciples' relationship with the Eternal passed through the physical presence of their master? The answer is no, absolutely not! You take God to be a person, a name and form. Name and form is what Jesus referred to as "the temple" when he said, "I am able to destroy the temple of God, and to build it in three days."[4] But the temple with which he identified is not the bearded man everyone thinks of when they hear the name "Jesus"; he identified with "I Am," with the body of Christ. In this, he was following the teaching of the Hebrew sages, who advocated investing the light of the Spirit in the belief that "I Am" is God. This practice had long been revealed in the Jewish tradition, which is why the disciples should have been familiar with it. And yet when the storm started they were terrified of losing their lives. Had they been following the path of loving God, the immortal part of themselves would have freed them from the fear of death.

Like many of their contemporaries, the apostles had strayed from the path prescribed in the Old Testament: "I am returned unto Zion, and will dwell in the midst of Jerusalem: and Jerusalem shall be called a city of truth; and the mountain of the Lord of hosts the holy mountain."[5] "Zion" here refers to the temple of the human body, the precious instrument that enables us to see "I Am." It is this temple that gives us the feeling that we are witnessing the world, so the first step is to return to the sense of being a witness. Then, subjectively, "dwell in Jerusalem," which is synonymous with "I Am." At this stage, abide in His peace and praise the Lord. It is interesting to note that phonetically, "Jerusalem" in Hebrew means, "If you are inside, everything is God; if you are outside, there is nothing." "Jerusalem shall be called a city of truth": as your inner self matures, you are filled by the peace of the Almighty and the divine Spirit that you are is revealed. This is the path taught by the Hebrew prophets; it is the path that Jesus was born into and followed all his life, and that forms the very basis of his teaching.

When the Lord says, "Awake, awake, stand up, O Jerusalem, which hast drunk at the hand of the Lord the cup of his fury,"[6] he is not addressing you as a person: he is calling you "Jerusalem," the body of His peace, who is born again and who, by abiding in peace, awakens to the immortal, to "the Truth."

THE DIVINE MOTHER OF YOUR THOUGHTS

Q: Everything's fine when I'm on a retreat, but when I get home and find a little brown tax envelope on my doormat my heart sinks. I wish I could rise above it all—but then everyone has these sorts of problems. I know that Mā is always standing there beside me and that there is inner silence, and yet. . . .

A: The path of knowledge sets you free from fear but it takes time, patience, and perseverance. The world presents itself to you in a particular form on a particular day, but you decide not to accept it as it is: you want it to be different.

Q: But everyone's like that.

A: It is true that the vast majority of people are like that, and if you are too it shows that, like everyone else, you are a subject of His Royal Highness Fear! On the path to the divine Self, you have to be prepared to accept any situation as an expression of His will. If it is His will that you lose your house or your car, say to Him, "Fine. If that's your will, so be it. It's your affair."

Life stretches out ahead of you and you do not know what the future holds. You have practiced remaining in the presence of Mā at the level of thought and you experience the silence that emerges from your innermost Self as a sense of the unknown. That silence is Her, Mā, the divine Mother. Put your trust in Her. All you need do is sit on her lap and "sacrifice"[7] yourself to Her; let yourself be held by Her. Inner silence, which is the fruit of your practice, flows from the Infinite. She and He are one. Silence is the tangible form in which God appears, manifested as the Mother who protects, guides, and comforts you. The divine Mother of your thoughts who stands beside you, who is outside you, was a necessary practice at the beginning. Now it is important to identify with silence rather than with your thoughts. Apply your image of Her to the silence that is growing in you.

Q: She has no dimension.

A: At the beginning She is limited to whatever dimension your thoughts give Her; but that is not enough, because all dimensions are within Her. The Mother standing beside you was a necessary stage at the start of your journey. Gradually let go of that prop now that She is emerging in the form of silence. Love Her in the form of silence, where She is the Infinite. And next time the little brown envelope drops on your doormat, you can either react with fear or put a childlike trust in sacredness, whose symbol is the Cross. In this childlike trust there is both the vulnerability of a newborn and invulnerability, because you are giving yourself up to Her. Lay your problems at Her feet and abandon all your fears.

THE ROLE OF RELIGION

Q: Since inner peace is the measure and since the path is through universal peace, what's the use of religion? Why does God seem to answer some people's prayers by granting them spiritual experiences and visions, and other people, who follow the same religion, claim to be "chosen" or "saved" and sometimes even go to war to assert their superiority?

A: Religion is supposed to bring people together. It should teach us to have the dignity of belonging to the divine body of inner peace; this is the only education that can build a humane society. All religions worship God under different names and forms, and these concrete concepts of "I Am" are useful because without them the concrete idea you have of yourself cannot abide in the abstract reality of "I Am." To the mind, "I Am" is abstract. You mistakenly identify with the concept of body and mind, and another concept is needed to remedy this, just as you would use a wooden toothpick to remove a bit of wood caught between your teeth.

A concept of God makes it possible to remain comfortably in the practice of "I Am" and be reborn. John the Baptist, baptizing with water, symbolizes man turning toward God and abiding in His presence, until the concept "I Am + an attribute" dissolves into "I Am." For people who respect the universal nature of the divine, the path can be Hindu, Hebrew, Christian, Muslim, or any other religious denomination.

Every religion advocates the repetition of the name of God or of a particular prayer. This is the most effective way of focusing the mind and practicing being in His presence, in the same way that a block of ice has to remain immersed in water for a long time before it dissolves. People today are impatient and want instant results. They are proud of their intellect and find it difficult to use a concept of God because they know that it is an elementary stage on the spiritual path. They would rather be given a practice that makes them feel they are skipping the early stages. Sooner or later, however, they realize that to abide in "I Am" in the midst of the chaos of daily life is impossible.

A concept of God provides you with an inner friend, which makes the practice of inner silence comfortable and prepares you for the baptism of fire, for the awakening to the Spirit. The divine and worshipful Spirit that transcends every point in space does not discriminate between different religious paths, it sustains them all. It is human beings, with their religious institutions built on egoic territories, who divide and try to conquer by proselytizing. The great sage Vivekananda said that the British had conquered India with the three B's: "Bible, Brandy, and Bayonets." Episodes of this kind are legion throughout history. But why let it impress you? Whatever impresses you leaves an imprint and condemns you to return and relive the cosmic dream. The entire history of humankind, from age immemorial and in every part of the world, is contained in the here and now of "I Am" and has no more importance than a puff of smoke.

SUFFERING AND EVOLUTION

Q: Why are human beings caught up in this cycle of suffering? Is it the will of God?

A: No! It is the divine Spirit that you are that chooses to play the game, the *lila*,[8] of God. Wake up and you will realize that all your incarnations were just so many delusions, that they never happened—like a wave that had believed in the world of waves, with its names, forms, geographical, historical, and social relationships, and one day realizes the great truth: there is only water.

On the relative plane, every atom in the universe is evolving toward its source, toward the Infinite. On our planet, the vegetable world evolved where billions of years before there had been nothing but the burning gases of stars. You are God asleep when you exist in the form of a stone, God dreaming when in animal form, and God awakening when you obtain a human life. The long transformation that produced trees, flowers, and animals came about without suffering because nature evolves in harmony with "I Am" and partakes, therefore, in the fullness of the Infinite. Because nature lives in tune with its substratum, it never leaves the Garden of Eden. But humans, who do not live in harmony with interiority, create an imbalance that causes terrible suffering. This suffering is an expression of "I Am," which forces us, for our greatest good, to return to our true home.

Fear greatly increases suffering. If you believe in the external world, your imagination feeds your fear and you can dream up anything in the world of name and form. If you live the dream as though it were reality, you live disconnected from life and the consequences are extremely painful.

Q: Has evolution come to an end?

A: No, because even if they are not conscious of it, human beings are an integral part of nature. Their ignorance and misdeeds cause terrible suffering but evolution goes on. Inevitably, at some point, people's hearts soften and, eventually, one day they say, "Enough! I want to go home!" This is a sign that the dream is drawing to an end and it marks the zenith of evolution. At that point, people discover what came before this universe, before even the sense of "I Am," and they understand that all those billions of years were but a split second compared with eternity. They discover where they are one with God and that they have always been free.

THE ORIGIN OF SUFFERING

Q: When there's a catastrophe like the shipwreck of the *Titanic*, or an earthquake or a tsunami, where many people die at the same time, is it collective karma?

A: There is indeed individual and collective karma. In Cambodia, for example, the Khmer Rouge, who massacred millions of people, will eventually be reborn. They will come back into the world together and will die together, murdered as they themselves murdered. We tend to look only at the people who suffer but we should not forget those who inflict suffering.

Q: The Bible talks of original sin. What is the state of sin and to what extent is it responsible for evil?

A: At the level of the body of flesh and blood, sin exists as soon as you seize "I Am" and label it, as in "I am the color of my skin." At the level of thought, sin exists as soon as you grasp and elaborate the concept "my," "your," "his," "their," as in "my" opinion or "your" nationality. This creates an egoic territory in which life manifests as desire and this expresses itself as "I want." The teaching that frees you from sin is, in the words of Christ: "Render to God the things that are God's." That is to say, give "I Am" back to God.

Understand that "I Am," which is simply your sense of soul, your sense of interiority, is God. When you limit "I Am" by saying "I am this" or "I am that," your actions inevitably arise from ignorance. Love and belief invested in a certain idea automatically lead to certain actions, which are predetermined and leave no room for free will. This is a law of nature, and when you see it in operation in the wild no one is surprised. Take, for example, an old lion and a lioness that has just given birth to cubs. If a young male comes along and chases the old lion away, the young lion's first reaction will be to kill the old lion's cubs in order to ensure his own lineage. If he does not, the lioness will be busy with her cubs and show no interest in the young male.

The egoic territory keeps people prisoner of these natural laws and leads them to commit terrible acts, such as murder, looting, and rape. Because they believe in a certain idea, people automatically behave in a certain way, and the stronger their attachment to the idea, the more extreme their actions. This is the root cause of all suffering, because eventually people have to undergo the same suffering that they have inflicted.

Humans have an overblown sense of their own importance—out of all proportion to reality. In relation to the universe our world is as insignificant as an ants' nest. As long as people remain confined within the narrow limits of their humanity, all wars, problems, and suffering are no more important than the suffering of an insect. On the scale of the universe, they are a non-event. Conversely, when you make room in your life for God in the form of "I Am," the universe itself is as insignificant as a puff of smoke in relation to the "I Am" with which you are then aligned.

Q: Wouldn't it have been simpler if we had remained at the animal stage?

A: At the animal stage we were happy and were carried along by life, but animals are still part of the cosmic dream. There comes a time when you have to get out of the dream.

Q: Why?

A: Because it is just a dream! Knowing what you now know, would you want to return to being a dog?

Q: Definitely not!

A: Of course not. Something in you understands that there is an evolutionary current that compels you to leave the dream and return to the Infinite, to reality, to your true home, where suffering no longer prevails. Indeed, for you to be sitting here now listening to these words, you must already have traveled a long way as a human being. Depending on the intensity with which you practice what has been shared here with you, this birth can be your last. You are still young. Picture where you want to be at the moment of death. Do you want to be where you are now? Wouldn't you rather be fully awakened, anchored in the Spirit, and ready to depart this life like the sages for whom death is the happiest moment because the glory of the Infinite is restored to them? You can if you want. It isn't that complicated!

Everyone has to decide for themselves. Even if your efforts are not rewarded on the human plane, any effort you make in the direction of God is never wasted. Never.

THERE IS MORE TO THE WORLD THAN YOUR WORLDLINESS

Your heart is completely taken up with world events: a war here, social conflict there, political and economic problems, sporting events, love affairs of actors and pop singers—a flood of information of all kinds has seeped into your inner space and occupies it.

Is this really what the world is? Do the events happening on our planet, even taken in their entirety, really make up "reality"? A newspaper recently published a photograph of space taken from Mars. In the center of the photo is a small arrow with the caption "You Are Here!" The tip of the arrow points to a tiny blue dot: us, planet Earth, seen from our neighboring planet Mars. From Pluto, Earth would not even be visible—let alone from another galaxy. Try to find Earth among the many billions of suns and solar systems! Seen from this perspective, Earth could disappear and the rest of the universe would be unaffected. Dinosaurs died out and the universe goes on. Stars are born and die every day without us even being aware of it.

The world is so much more than your worldliness. The entire sum of events taking place on Earth, from the most sublime to the most terrible, is but a trifle on the scale of the universe.

Soon after Independence, the president of India paid a visit to the great sage of the Himalayas, Swami Sivananda. After Partition, Hindus were leaving Pakistan to return to India and Muslims were leaving India for Pakistan. It was a difficult time, and the president set out a long list of his problems before the great sage, who listened patiently. When he had finished, Swami Sivananda simply said: "Seen from the state I am in, everything you have told me is no more important than a puff of smoke."

Why did he say this? Because all the galaxies and universes are but a grain of sand in the infinity of God, in the infinity of "I Am," and it was with this that Swami Sivananda was aligned. You believe that the world is external to you, when in fact it is within God, within His peace. The truth is that "I Am" is in charge of the universe and not human beings, who cannot even be sure of their next breath.

Swami Sivananda was anchored in the Infinite and bore witness on earth to divine love. He built hospitals and schools, and lived his whole life in the service of all. Even today, long after his death, his life inspires people to awaken and serve, which is the paradox of a life dedicated to God rather than to humanity.

THE ROLE OF NATURE

Q: What role does nature play on the path to awakening?

A: Everyone loves nature. It is an expression of "I Am," which is why its many different forms touch our soul—be it mountains, birdsong, the sea, the setting sun, the scent of damp earth, or the rustle of wind in the leaves.

If, however, your enjoyment of nature does not extend beyond identifying with your senses, you remain separate from what you are enjoying and that is not enough. You must see nature as an integral part of interiority, in which you acknowledge the fact of God, so that it becomes no longer "your" ears that hear but "I Am," no longer "your" nose that smells but "I Am," and when you gaze at a beautiful landscape it is no longer "your" eyes that see but the eyes of God.

Q: Can I use nature as a concept of God?

A: It is an interesting idea, but there is a danger of remaining trapped in likes and dislikes. You like birds and flowers but you dislike rats, flies, spiders, and anything that crawls. Yet these creatures are as much part of "I Am" as the ones you like. They are just as important as birds and flowers, because at the level of God or "I Am" there are no preferences. When something in nature appeals to you, it touches you at the level of inner peace and, because when you like something it reveals to you the sense of "I Am," it can help you remain effortlessly connected to interiority. This is a step in the right direction. But a frequent mistake is to imagine that the peace you experience when you look at a landscape, for example, comes from the landscape itself. This confers a power on the "object" that it obviously does not possess.

For this reason it is important to recognize the universal nature of interiority. What standpoint should you adopt in order for interiority to include everyone and everything? This is where the word "God" comes in. You can equally well use the word "life," on condition that for you the word contains the intelligence of the Infinite, which is to say an intelligence that speaks to you, guides you, helps, comforts, and, above all, leads you back to your true Self. In which case, what difference is there with the word "God"?

You are like a wave that is being asked to recognize that interiority is the tangible expression of the ocean. The ocean, which includes all waves and awakens each wave to its "oceanity," is called, at the human level, "God." For a wave that has returned to its true nature, the word "God" falls away. He, the immortal and infinite Being, IS, and you are That.

Q: Is the experience of God identical to what you experience when you're by the sea or in the desert? I spent two years in Tunisia and I felt something very powerful happen to me there.

A: An experience is just an experience and, in itself, is of no importance. It is only significant insofar as it reveals to you where you are one with the Infinite. You interpret your experience in the desert as coming from the desert itself, which I call the "parasitical attitude." What in fact happens when you love something is that your mind is reduced to silence. This produces a state of deep peace and that is why you experienced something powerful and unexpected. At this point, ask yourself, "Who sees this?"

Q: I don't understand how you can say that an experience is of no importance.

A: In the Bhagavad Gita, Lord Krishna revealed himself to Arjuna in all His infinite names and forms, in the most wondrous vision that a human can behold. This manifestation of the Almighty was too much for Arjuna and he implored Krishna to return to his usual form. Ramana Maharshi, the great sage of Arunachala, said that Arjuna had had the vision because it was already present in his spirit. By this he meant that your true being is greater than any experience you might undergo; more important than any vision you might have. The Almighty is an ocean of infinite love that wants only to restore you to the glory of absolute beatitude. His will is constantly expressing itself through you in the form of life, through the sense of "I Am" in interiority.

Once the euphoria of the experience was over, Arjuna was still Arjuna and he still identified with himself as a person. The vision reinforced his faith, but a vision is not enough. Suppose that because of your experience you had decided to settle in the Tunisian desert, and twenty years later you realized that your life was still unfulfilled, that it still lacked something. Things would not have worked out the way you imagined.

Your mistake is to think that an experience of the divine is addressed to you as a person. Any interpretation based on this misunderstanding is bound to be wrong. Look at what happened during the Crusades when a pious French king, who ruled over a peaceful country, had a profound mystical experience that he interpreted as a call from God to deliver Jerusalem. He emptied his coffers, gathered up his army, and set off to war. A few years later he came back a sick and ruined man, his kingdom plunged into famine and misery. This kind of event has happened again and again—and goes on happening today.

It is not that your experience of peace is unimportant, but that you interpret it as a way of giving meaning to your life as a person. In reality, the purpose of life and all its manifestations is to lead you to find the answer to the questions: Who am I? Who sees the experience?

Understand that God's only wish is to restore you to supreme happiness, to what you truly are. Whether He manifests as a profound experience or as an absence, your job is to put your faith in Him. The purpose of life is to reveal to you where you are one with the Spirit, with the Eternal. Your highest duty is to live with this conviction.

TOTALITY AND LOCALITY

Q: When you listen to the news, it's difficult to believe that the world is absolutely perfect. How is it possible to remain indifferent to all the terrible things that are happening?

A: What is happening that is imperfect? Show me something imperfect.

Q: For me, what is imperfect is that the imperfections of the world still disturb me; I'm frightened of terrorist attacks, wars, and so on.

A: So what is imperfect is your fear! No one has tried to shoot you, have they? And yet you are frightened of it happening.

Q: I know it's an illusion, but. . . .

A: If someone tries to shoot you, I doubt you'll say it is an illusion! But for you, right now, where is the problem?

Q: In my mind.

A: Exactly! It is in your imagination. You have invested the light of your belief in mental images that feed your fears. Your assertion that you are a person is the basic problem; the assertion of the sages that you are Spirit is the solution to the problem. The world is perfect because it is an expression of the totality of "I Am," which in itself is perfect. You have invested your light in believing that you belong to the world of form, to a specific locality, and by connecting yourself to a locality you are disconnected from totality. It is locality that makes you believe that things are imperfect, whereas totality is perfect.

This disconnection, which comes from believing in names and forms, is the source of your troubles. It is you, light of the divine Spirit, who is responsible for the heaven or hell you experience on earth, and not some god or devil in your mind. By investing the light of the Eternal in a love of names and forms, you endow them with a quality of truth they do not possess and, in this way, you create a whole cinema of likes and dislikes. This cinema can drive people to acts of extreme cruelty, the consequences of which they will have to endure through an infernal cycle of deaths and rebirths. These will only come to an end when they decide to go back home. Jesus said that each of us is rewarded, in an exact measure, according to our actions. This is why the scriptures state that the world is an expression of perfect justice.

Human beings behave as though they were the center of the universe, and the only thing that matters to them is what is happening in their world. The imperfections you refer to concern the human world. In relation to the universe, the world of politicians, society, the media, technology—whatever it may be—are of no importance whatsoever. Humans are as much part of nature as every other species; no more, no less.

The problems you perceive are rarely connected to the events themselves, but derive from fear. If, for example, you are frightened of flying and have to take a nine-hour flight, whenever the plane hits turbulence you are going to imagine that there is a problem with the engines. Then the flight goes smoothly and the plane lands without a hitch, so what was the problem? The problem was that you sat consumed with fear for nine hours about something you imagined! The antidote to this is to trust God with all your heart in all circumstances, even when your life is in the balance.

SCIENCE AND REALITY

Q: You said that the cosmos works through us. . . .

A: No, I never said that!

Q: But we're part of cosmic evolution, since we are made up of matter.

A: We are not matter! We are not this body of flesh and blood.

Q: At a cellular level, at the level of DNA . . .

A: DNA is part of the physical world.

Q: It's something we can see.

A: Just because we can measure certain "objects" and reproduce them in experiments, we think we understand the world. But our understanding is limited by the subject-object nature of scientific methods and we miss the essential. If you want to understand the nature of the world, you must go within, to the life inside you, which cannot be perceived as an object but is reality, your essential being. Scientists will never discover the essence of matter by studying the external world; they will never discover the "God particle."

Q: What about our biological makeup?

A: You talk about "our" biology as if you owned it! Does it belong to you?

Q: It isn't mine personally, but as a human being. . . .

A: A human being is just a wider concept. It is what you think you are because you identify with body, name, and form. But that is not what you are!

Q: Human beings spend their lives trying to understand and explain reality through science. Are we wasting our time?

A: Studying the physical world can be helpful or harmful, depending on what use the results are put to. But as far as reality, the essence of the world, is concerned, scientists lag far behind. This reality has been known for thousands of years and has been revealed to saints and sages of every tradition. In India, the essence of the world is known as *hiranyagarbha,* which is synonymous with "I Am" or with the state of the world before creation. Just as before waves there was water, so before creation there was "I Am." It is the substratum of the universe; it is what Jesus referred to when he said, "Before Abraham was, I am."[9] He was referring to that great subjective reality with which he identified. For this reason, the knowledge of someone such as St. Francis of Assisi, who lived nearly a thousand years ago, is infinitely superior to that of any scientist, past or present. St. Francis's knowledge was based on his experience of inner reality, which is existence, the heart of life itself.

How can the intellect understand itself or understand the nature of the universe? Can a wave understand the ocean? It can try for all eternity but it will never succeed. Our so-called science is like a wave in the world of name and form, limited by logic, by the subject-object relationship, and by time and space. In the sacred texts of India, which are based on the direct experience of sages, the entire universe, time, space, life, and what appears to be death, are nothing but a ripple of "I Am." Now that is a beautiful science!

KARMA

Q: I don't understand what karma is.

A: Karma can be summed up as: "You reap what you sow."

Q: Does it apply to past or future actions?

A: What's the difference?

Q: I understand about the future, and I'm sure my future karma will be better. But the past?

A: How can you accept one without acknowledging the other?

Q: I don't understand.

A: Are you sure it's a lack of understanding?

Q: I feel a certain resistance. . . .

A: To what?

Q: I don't understand what I've done to God to deserve all the suffering I've had to endure. I can't admit that I'm responsible.

A: In other words, you think that God has made a mistake?

Q: Yes, I do!

A: You consider yourself to be an innocent victim?

Q: The resistance comes from the fact that some people tell me I'm responsible and yet all my life I've been considered a victim. I've even been designated a "war victim." My mother was also a "war victim" and the expression has been inseparable from my family for many years. This is why I can't accept the idea that I'm responsible. It's a big obstacle!

A: I understand. But the term "war victim" is just a definition superimposed on events that you have lived through—there is nothing unusual there. But you have identified with the definition, as if the events you experienced are who you are. I part company with you there: you are the light of the divine Spirit and not the events that make up your life or the person who lived through them.

When you are at the movies, the projector gives a semblance of truth to the moving images. In the same way, the light of the Eternal wrongly projected onto the images and definitions of the world endows them with an apparent quality of truth. The result of this mistake is called karma. This is how you, the light of the Eternal, fall into the karma trap, because this world is governed by inescapable laws, such as the law of action and reaction. When you identify with the images of the world instead of with its essence, with "I Am," you are automatically subject to these laws. This is not the case for sages, as Jesus demonstrated when he said to Pontius Pilate, "My kingdom is not of this world."[10]

I have a friend in California whose whole family was massacred at Auschwitz. He is the sole survivor. An experience such as this undeniably leaves deep scars in every cell of your body, yet there is no wound that the light of the Eternal cannot heal. My friend met Swami Sivananda, the great sage of the Himalayas. He followed the path prescribed by the sages of India and is now reconciled with God. What was possible for him is possible for you.

Q: I'm sure it is. It's the word "resistance" that I found difficult to say aloud.

A: The visceral connection you have with your family history and your past sustains your belief that the cinema of life is real. We have all, at some point, made that mistake. But as soon as you recognize that you are here, in God in the form of peace, the direction of your life changes. You go back home and all those you love are also blessed by His peace.

THE EGOIC TERRITORY AND UNHAPPINESS

The natural movement of life flows to the Infinite. Identification with the body, which produces the desire to look for happiness through the senses, creates an opposite movement that flows toward the external world. It is when these two movements converge that you experience unhappiness and boredom.

The person you think you are—an accumulation of attributes you have superimposed on "I Am"—is not real. But the feelings that arise when the natural movement of life meets the opposite current, the egoic territory, are real, and manifest as unhappiness, an impersonal force that invites you to change course and discover your true nature, which is bliss. To achieve this, you must live in communion with the will of God, in connection with interiority and with simple recognition of the divine in this interiority. You then realize that everything and everyone you meet is an expression of life, just as waves are an expression of the ocean.

The faith Jesus described as "no larger than a mustard seed" is precisely that of believing that "I Am," which is your sense of soul, is God. The "mountain" Jesus refers to is the accumulation of your identifications, concepts, and opinions. Obviously you cannot live and act in the world of duality without using ideas and concepts, but the mistake is to cling to them and allow them to crystallize, thereby restricting the natural flow of life.

The fundamental teaching is the following: recognize that interiority is holy ground, that it is the inexpressible reality we call God in which everything is included, in particular everything in your immediate surroundings. When you live in this way, in harmony with life, unhappiness goes out of your life forever. A simple birdsong is enough to make you happy, because your nature is bliss and you are on earth to be revealed to your true nature.

WANTING GOD AND GOD ALONE

Q: I do want God and God alone, but I can't add "to the exclusion of everything else."

A: At the beginning, the wave cannot imagine itself as anything but a wave. It has a sense of water but thinks, "It is my water"—in other words, "my soul," "my existence," and this implies "otherness." Then one day, another wave says to it, "You know, it isn't your wave, because water is universal. In your capacity as water, you are one with the ocean."

Believing in the reality of names and forms creates a feeling of separateness, of "me" and "others." In reality, there are no "others." To understand this, meditate deeply on the words of the scriptures: "All is God." You can also use a concrete idea of God and recognize that your sense of soul is, for example, the Immaculate Conception. You then realize that the things you hold so dear are all here, in Her, and the person you believe you are on the human plane is also contained in this universal reality.

This practice brings you into communion with life, and gives you a new self with the dignity of being the body of His peace. And then, in the words of St. Paul, "I live; yet not I, but Christ liveth in me." When you live in this way, you are freed from "my, yours, his, hers, theirs" and life begins to reveal its secrets, the greatest of which is "Only God Is."

As a child, I often imagined leaving home with my belongings tied into a small bundle on the end of a stick and setting off, alone with God. I imagined myself sitting by a lake or walking in a forest with the feeling "I'm free!" and this filled me with intense joy. Today, I have realized my childhood dream. This absolute freedom is that of the Spirit. If you make it the purpose of your life, to the exclusion of everything else, the world is yours; if not, you receive merely its reflections. To abide in this fullness is the only worthwhile goal in life.

Q: How do you know when you're established in renunciation?

A: Suppose someone in this room says to you, "That's a really stupid question!" If you are the least bit affected by the remark, it shows that you are still looking for something in the world, and traces of "I want" remain. If this is the case, be aware of it, and say to yourself, "my inner reaction proves that I'm not really anchored in 'I want God and God only, to the exclusion of everything else.'" Realize you feel that something is still lacking and try to find where you can be free in relation to the person who made the remark. In this way, you develop awareness, particularly where the state of freedom is concerned. It is about being free from other people's opinions that largely condition our behavior, and of abiding in the conviction, "I am one with God." In this way, you are always turned toward Him.

THE EGOIC TERRITORY AND "I WANT"

Q: "I want to invest my light in the right direction" and "All I want is God and God alone," aren't these manifestations of an egoic territory?

A: "I want" is an impersonal force that does not belong to you; it is a current that results from how you have invested your love and belief. Before "I want" comes "I love." When you love God in the form of "I Am," you realize that interiority is a sacred place and that every form of life is His expression. Your life then becomes the current "I want God," which enables you to discover, in the here and now, where you are one with the Infinite. In this state, which is universal, how can there be room for an egoic territory?

But if you have invested your light in the love of money, cars, jewels, or such, you believe that happiness depends on these things, and the current "I want" pulls you outward in order to satisfy these illusory needs.

Your nature is plenitude, and the state of inner peace already contains everything you are looking for in the external world. Wanting God and God alone, to the exclusion of anything else, is the highest goal. It may seem paradoxical, but when you put this into practice your life on earth manifests a wisdom and goodness that are not of this world.

MANIFESTATIONS OF GOD AND FAITH

There is a great reality that is both transcendent and immanent, of which the universe is but an infinitesimal expression. This great and adorable reality is generally called "God." It is present in our hearts in the form of "I Am," which is the sense of existence as each one of us experiences it. But because you think of yourself as a concrete person, it is hard to remain in this abstract reality, particularly since the experience of interiority is often accompanied by a feeling of expansion, which can be frightening for a beginner.

To make it possible to remain easily and comfortably immersed in inner reality, God appears on earth in the concrete form of apparitions. These always respect religious traditions, at the same time as delivering teachings of the highest order. Why, for example, is the statue of the Virgin of Montserrat black? When you shut your eyes and look within at "I Am," you are confronted with darkness and the unknown. That darkness is Her. The apparition of the Virgin reveals that what you interpret as "your experience," "your soul," is in fact Her. As soon as you recognize this, the way you usually perceive the world is turned upside down and you realize that what you had thought was "your" experience is, in fact, universal. These apparitions provide us with a concrete idea of God that helps us abide in the abstract reality.

Q: When you look within, you see light and sometimes a presence or a force.
A: These are impressions created by the prism of your identification with the person. They can be part of the path, and meditating on the attributes of God, for example, is helpful. But there is more. Put aside your ideas about God for a minute and concentrate on what is really there. Try to sense

interiority without interfering with the experience in any way. Abandon all mental interpretations. In that moment, when everything comes to a stop, know that God is there. What do you feel now?

Q: An inexpressible, holy state.

A: Exactly! The difficulty is to make it last.

Q: How do you make it last?

A: It is impossible for you, as a person, to "do" anything to make the state last. The answer lies in the idea you have of yourself. Your attitude should be: "It is not I who speaks, but," for example, "Christ." "It is not I who hears, sees, or thinks, but Christ." In this way, the intelligence of the Infinite and the concept of personal intelligence—which is the result of false identification with the intellect—are reconciled. What is your state, as it is, at this moment?

Q: A holy state!

A: Exactly! If you try to grasp the state, it will always elude you. But you are always there for yourself—it isn't easy to forget yourself! So it is important to begin with what you are identified with at the moment. You cannot concentrate on your work and this holy state at the same time, but you can live with the dignity of being the body of His peace. This is why manifestations of God can be helpful. Choose whichever one gives your mind a place to pause and rest. This holy state is always there for you and it can help you keep in mind the dignity of belonging to His peace. Then one day, it will become so natural that you can let go of any props. At every moment of your life, your attitude should be: "It is not I who am doing but Thee, it is not I who am doing but Thee, it is not I who am doing but Thee."

ELIMINATING THE INDIVIDUAL

Q: I don't understand how you can eliminate personality in order to attain a higher level of consciousness. We go through life, from childhood to adolescence and adulthood, with the help of our intelligence. Consciousness develops naturally as we gradually detach ourselves. Does attaining the absolute, universal "I" happen in the same way?

A: What do you want in life?

Q: That's just it, it changes all the time!

A: There is the problem. Where are you truly yourself? Do you really know yourself?

Q: At some level.

A: At what level do you situate "I"?

Q: It depends.

A: There is, in fact, only one "I." But you can neither find it nor understand it through the prism of identification with the intellect. What you really are is divine Spirit and you are That for all eternity. But until you, the light of the Eternal, decide to go back home, God can do nothing. You are the keeper of the bubble of your dream, and at the moment, apparently, you are following your own path and your own way of thinking.

The path to knowing the Self is clear, scientific, and precise. It is not to be undertaken in the way you want, but in the manner prescribed by sages for thousands of years: *"asato ma sad gamaya,"* "lead me from the unreal to the real."

Q: I don't understand how you can completely eliminate the individual, with all its drives and desires.

A: You are still talking at a human level. I am talking about the Infinite, the Eternal, of which this universe is but an infinitesimal expression. The individual you refer to did not exist before you were born, will not exist after the death of the body, and disappears every night during deep sleep. In deep sleep, the world vanishes, along with the individual you think you are. You die to the world, whatever might have happened during the day. Even if you have been through the most terrible suffering, nothing is left in deep sleep, not even a sense of God. And yet you are there and you can wake up in the morning and say, "I've been asleep."

The world of name and form is an expression of "I Am," and "I Am" emerges from the state of deep sleep just as a spider's web emerges from the spider's body. By practicing abiding in "I Am," you ripen to inner peace, and there you can see that "I Am" includes the world of name and form, just as water includes the world of waves. You have fully ripened when you can recognize the state of deep sleep in the waking state. At that point, the apparent difference between the "I-thought" and the sense of "I Am" disappears.

This state, called ishvara, is indescribable, because it is inaccessible to the intellect. When you find "I," you have attained the highest level of spiritual knowledge, although "attain" is incorrect since "I" cannot be attained but is revealed. The only term you can apply here is "Spirit." The Spirit cannot be an object of experience in the usual sense, just as awareness cannot be felt as an experience. It is the Spirit in each of us that understands the words "My Father and I are one" and "Only God Is."

GOD ALSO MANIFESTS AS ABSENCE

Q: It bothers me that I can't make room for inner peace. The harder I try, the more difficult it gets. It's a vicious circle!

A: It is inevitable at the beginning, but with practice and perseverance you will succeed. Think carefully about the direction your life is going in and realize that time is a precious gift. Ripening in peace requires patience and persistence. You can only give yourself to it fully when you have truly decided to awaken in this lifetime, which is why it is important to make God the purpose of your life and constantly practice abiding in His presence.

Q: Even when you can't feel it?

A: Who can feel the presence of God? Only those who believe in it and who practice the belief. God is always present. Your experience, whatever it may be, is His way of expressing himself in you. The difference between what you feel or do not feel depends entirely on what you believe; if you do not believe in His presence, you feel a void and this opens the way to doubt and despair. But if you practice believing that He is there, in your experience as it is, His fullness gradually unfolds. But you have to be patient. What does "feeling the presence of God" mean to you?

Q: Perhaps I didn't express myself very well.

A: You did, but you are probably under the impression that feeling the presence of God is necessarily associated with inner peace. That is a misconception. God is there in the form of peace but also as absence. He manifests as stillness but also as distress and inner turmoil. Learn to love Him in either case. That which sees Him in both presence and absence is above both; you are the light of the Eternal that reveals itself when you have faith in

His presence and His absence. Only you can choose to shine your light in this way and decide to trust Him with all your heart. It then becomes evident that He Is. Fear and stress do not disappear overnight, but if you abide in the practice of the presence of God, fear gradually makes way for great peace and suffering leaves your life forever. But be careful: practicing in order to eliminate suffering and to be in peace is not enough, and is contrary to the path prescribed by the sages. You must make God the purpose of your life. This is the highest and only worthwhile goal.

Q: I understand, but what if the problem persists?

A: The problem comes from an egoic territory, which itself is the result of your light invested in concepts such as "my" son, "my" daughter, "my" country, into which you have placed all your love and affection. In a sense, you have made them into false gods. It is love invested in an egoic territory that generates emotions, disturbs your peace of mind, and is responsible for your present state. You want peace, but you also want many other things. In these circumstances, it is not possible to see and act wisely or well. If you want to help yourself and others, your actions must be grounded in inner peace. Give up wanting anything and make your prayer, "Lord, grant me the serenity to accept the things I cannot change, courage to change the things I can, and wisdom to know the difference."

At this stage, repeating the name of God is your best means of ripening in His peace. His light will shine in your life, gradually healing even the deepest wounds from the past and freeing you from all your fears. Whether or not you feel peace is of no importance. Trust Him with all your heart and know that you are free.

HOW TO STOP JUDGING

Q: How can we avoid the endless judgments we make in life? In all our relationships, we're always judging the other person: he's like this, she's like that; I like him, I don't like her.

A: You have touched there on one of the subtlest elements that bind us to the world of name and form. There are many ways of not judging, but in essence the method is always the same: practice seeing God in every manifestation of His creation. This may seem simple, but putting it into practice is far from easy. Everything that impresses you leaves its imprint and is colored by your judgment. One effective way is to meditate on the state of the world before creation. Before creation, there is "I Am." It requires an effort of imagination, but the state itself is real. It is God in whatever form you choose to represent Him. This whole universe is nothing but an infinitesimal expression of that adorable reality, which is not in your hands but His. This includes your nearest and dearest, however much the closeness of your relationship with them might make you think otherwise.

The good news is that we are all one and, sooner or later, everyone decides to go back home. But the point at which you make the decision depends not on you but on the light of the Spirit in each one of us when, battered by life and fed up with suffering, we yearn for the bliss of the Infinite.

There is nothing to judge because there is no action, however vile, that we are incapable of committing. We are conditioned by our birth, upbringing, and environment, and it is only when we make room in our lives for God that we free ourselves from this conditioning and find the strength to transcend human drives and desires. As the saying goes, "Charity begins at home." When you abide in the presence of God, His peace ripens in you and you grow increasingly aware of the dignity conferred on you by belonging to His peace. The greater this sense of dignity, the more you realize that others share in it too. In this peace we are all one. If you judge people, however, it implies that you believe yourself to be separate, which is one of the subtlest obstacles between you and Self-knowledge.

During all my years in the blessed presence of my master, Swami Chidananda, my duty as a disciple was to see only God in him, just as he had done with his master, Swami Sivananda. According to Indian tradition, the disciple ignores the human aspect of the spiritual guide and focuses exclusively on the spiritual dimension. I had the opportunity, therefore, of being able to practice withholding judgment on someone who inspired the deepest love and respect in me. I was then able to extend this to everyone I met, and that is what enabled the Infinite to emerge in my life.

SURRENDERING TO GOD

Q: Isn't fear a lack of surrender to the will of God? When you surrender to God, you're no longer afraid.

A: What do you understand by "surrender to God"?

Q: That "Your will be done."

A: But what about you, where are you in that case? Surrendering to God is to acknowledge with every breath that God does everything. There is no question of you doing anything at all. From the point of view of water, the world of waves is nothing but shadow play. In the same way, the world, which seems so real to those who believe in concepts such as "I am a man" or "I am a woman," is, from the point of view of God in the form of "I Am," no more than a puppet show. When you understand this clearly, you have surrendered to God. If you think, "I am surrendering to God," then the individual you think you are is still there.

Q: Doesn't "Your will be done" and "God does everything" mean the same thing?

A: Yes, but "I am surrendering to God" is different. In that case you are still there as a person—and you are surplus to requirement! Seek refuge in God in the form of "I Am" and live with the conviction, "It is not I who sees, but 'I Am,' it is not I who remembers, but 'I Am.'" You will discover that we are all one and that God does not exist as an "other."

GOD IS THE BEST THERAPIST

Q: Do you think it's necessary to get psychological help in order to heal wounds from the past?

A: Doctors, psychiatrists, and psychotherapists all have their role to play in the world, but they cannot control nature. Their knowledge and experience enable them to help people, if they remain realistic and humble about what they know and what they can actually achieve. They cannot bring about a complete cure; only the light of God heals completely.

If a patient has been raped, for example, a psychotherapist can listen and try to help on a conscious and subconscious plane. This will procure real but only partial benefit. If, on the other hand, the patient makes room for interiority and recognizes the presence of God in that space, the light of the Spirit arises and gradually restores him or her to wholeness. When you learn to dwell in peace, the light of the Absolute manifests and heals even the deepest wounds. It cleanses the depths of the soul and washes away all negative residue, even that which comes from the distant past.

What human beings cannot heal, the light of God can, on condition that the person concerned turns away from the egoic territory to the path of awakening to the Spirit. Obviously, if you continually consult a psychologist because of past suffering, it may be because the egoic territory is looking for reinforcement at a psychological level: the complexity of psychology allows you to go on being a person, and can even reinforce your mountain of identifications. Seek help when you need it, but no permanent prop will ever bring about a cure.

If you follow the path of awakening to the Self, your faith in God must be absolute, regardless of how He manifests in the cinema of your life. There is no room for doubt or despair.

SELF-KNOWLEDGE AND PSYCHOTHERAPY

Q: Can we ever have true knowledge of the person we think we are?

A: True knowledge is knowing who you really are. The person you believe yourself to be is not who you are. So your question comes down to: "Can I have true knowledge of the person I believe myself to be, but who I am not?" You might as well try to discover, when you are dreaming, whether you have true knowledge of the person you believe yourself to be in the dream!

Q: Can psychotherapy lead to Self-knowledge?

A: Can you know the true Self through psychotherapy? Certainly not; it would imply that psychotherapy is greater than God. The path to the Eternal is through "I Am," of which psychotherapy is but a part, and not the other way round. It is an instrument on the path but not the path itself. "I Am" is the path.

Nor can you find the Self through mechanical thought processes, which is why psychotherapy as taught at universities cannot lead to Self-knowledge. It is nevertheless important to understand the psychology of the egoic territory and the drives that control human behavior. As an analogy, look at the animal kingdom. It is full of violence, a violence that is neither accept-able nor reprehensible: it is simply part of nature, so there is nothing to judge. A close study of the psychology and behavior of the animal kingdom reveals something that is rarely observable in the human world: a state of equilibrium.

When you study the psychology of the egoic territory, you find that the actions of people who live disconnected from life are always connected to an egoic territory. These territories make up the bubble of their dream, and once you understand how they function you no longer run the risk of get-ting caught up in other people's dreams. When a spiritual person is hurt or insulted, he or she usually struggles to find the right way of responding. Why not just allow the situation to be as it is and accept, without interfer-ing, the inner volcano that seems to demand an immediate reaction? An egoic territory acts according to its nature and you have to understand that insults are not personal but the product of an impersonal force. If you are driving your car and another driver insults you, that person's egoic territory is inviting you to react on the same level. Initially, you may find it hard to believe that it is possible to react in any way other than on the level of mind, but if in the moment, when you abstain from reacting, you think of God, you will find that there is a level on which you no longer react but can act.

There is a distinction, however, between insult and abuse. Everyone has the dignity of belonging to the divine, and this dignity should not be dragged through the mud because of a violent or abusive situation.

Psychotherapy is a useful but limited tool. A psychologist once said to Ma Anandamayi, "I try to help people solve their problems by talking to them, but you solve their problems without speaking!" The presence of someone established in the Infinite has an effect beyond anything that psy-chology can ever imagine.

Ma used to say, "Each to his own madness!" The best form of madness is to be mad for God.

ANGER

When a man thinks of objects, attachment to them arises;
From attachment desire is born; from desire anger arises.[11]

Love invested in an object makes you believe that happiness comes from that object. This gives rise to the urge "I want," a movement of life that is connected to an egoic territory and is characterized by desire and attachment. As soon as anything or anyone comes between you and the object, the movement expresses itself as anger. Given its strength, you usually find yourself overwhelmed by the emotion and incapable of standing back from the situation. To do so, you need to have practiced abiding in "I Am" and be familiar with the peace that lies at the heart of the practice. You can then identify the movement at its source and decide not to yield to it. This is where true free will resides. You, the Spirit, can decide whether to get caught up in the dream by giving in to anger, or whether to choose freedom and the Infinite. At that moment, a kind of opening occurs, an expansion, and That which sees the movement arising is the true "I." It is free from the bubble of the dream in which the anger arises, and free from the madness of other people's egoic territories. Be careful not to get caught up in other people's dreams!

At the beginning, it is natural for the process to be a little shaky, and you will discover a close link between anger and fear, but don't be afraid. When you decide to start walking toward the Infinite, you do not become passive but instead learn to act without losing sight of the dignity of the divine Spirit that you are. Where you are Spirit, there is Bhagavan, an ocean of infinite love, to which, through your actions, you bear witness in this world.

INCORPORATING DESIRE INTO PEACE

When you incorporate what you love into peace, you realize that you lose nothing and that a particular kind of joy arises.

Q: Does this also apply to desire?

A: What is desire if not the belief that an object, which is separate from you, will make you happy? The idea you have of being a man thinks, "To be happy, I need a woman." The idea you have of being poor thinks, "To be happy, I need money." Reflect on this carefully: it is the light of your being invested in the idea "I am this or that, man or woman, rich or poor" that creates your sense of being an individual, and this individual is inevitably associated with external objects and the sense organs. You can never satisfy desires that arise from your sense of belonging to the body of flesh and blood. On the other hand, all the women in the world and all the gold in the universe are there, in interiority. In "I Am" everything is yours, because you are one with all. As soon as you realize this, your mind becomes your ally. To find absolute joy, you must turn from the finite to the Infinite. This reveals where you are ananda, supreme bliss.

IDENTIFICATION WITH THE BODY

Q: You say that we should stop identifying with the body, but how do you go about it?

A: By practicing the presence of God and having the dignity of belonging to His peace while it ripens in you.

Q: But when suffering becomes unbearable, I don't see how it's possible.

A: The body is a prison that limits you in time and space. Being able to accept suffering, and even incorporate it into your daily practice, requires a good deal of courage. Do you love God in some form?

Q: Yes, in the form of Swami Sivananda.

A: That can be helpful. Saints have often been able to bear terrible pain by using an idea of God, an image of Christ, for example. Swami Sivananda was established in the Infinite and is now one with the divine Father, so to use him as an image of God is appropriate. At the end of his life, he suffered excruciating pain in his knees from arthritis and he endured it by ignoring it completely. You can practice being Swami Sivananda: your head is his head, your body his body, your condition his condition. Given his authenticity, if you lay your suffering on his suffering, it will gradually reveal to you where you are one with the Infinite.

Q: Do you have to have an image of God? Can't you just use peace and silence?

A: The peace you feel is an abstract reality. Your belief that you are a concrete person is not recent and, with time, it has crystallized. It can only dissolve when it has remained immersed long enough in the water of "I Am." Until then, the idea you have of being a person comes up against the difficulty of remaining in the abstract reality of "I Am." To overcome this difficulty, you need a concrete idea of God.

Look at the trees outside: do they belong to the peace you feel within?

Q: Yes.

A: Good. And is your consciousness an individual consciousness?

Q: Yes, it is.

A: An important step along the path to knowing the divine Self is to stop identifying with the mind, which is part of the physical body. The very nature of life is Consciousness, or that which in you is aware, and it is to this Consciousness that you must awaken. You must move from the level of human consciousness, which is created by the idea "I am human intelligence, for whom interiority is a personal experience," to a state of communion with interiority that is Consciousness. The sages of India are clear on this point: it is impossible to experience interiority as nirguna brahman, God in an abstract form, without going through saguna brahman, God as a personal concept. It is not so much the representation of a personal God that interests us, but the concrete support it gives to help us to become a body of peace. If I believe that the peace inside me is, for example, Christ, if I have loved everything connected with Jesus since I was a child and for me he is God, then it is easy to superimpose Christ on "I Am" and adopt the standpoint from which it is no longer I who sees but Christ, no longer I who speaks but Christ, no longer I who thinks but Christ. What I had thought was my personal, individual consciousness is, in fact, the very essence of life, with which I now live in harmony. The paradox is that I don't disappear, because I am That. You are That!

On the level of names and forms, it does not matter whether you choose Jesus or any other image. What matters is to familiarize yourself with the idea of an incarnated God and superimpose that idea on "I Am" until you can recognize that even the furthest stars are within you, here and now. You then spontaneously realize that your sense of individual consciousness is part of interiority. Do you understand? Faith no larger than a mustard seed is enough to send the whole mountain of personal pronouns—"mine," "yours," "his," "hers," "theirs," etc.—into the sea, together with the countless definitions that we impose on the truth.

BELIEF

The word "faith" is usually interpreted as the act of believing in God, a God that is often separate from you, living somewhere up in the sky. The Sanskrit word for faith, *shraddha,* is not easy to translate because it designates the act of trusting life and of believing in oneself, as well as a lot more still.

Can you live without belief? You can say, "I believe in God" or "I don't believe in God." But if you say you do not believe in God, with what do you believe your disbelief? The act of believing has no opposite. Like it or not, if you do not believe, you believe that you do not believe. At this very moment, you believe that it is daytime, that you are in a particular place at a particular time, that you are a man or woman, and that you are sitting down. Belief is there at every step. Belief is, in fact, an act of the Spirit.

The question to ask yourself is this: Where do you invest the light of the Spirit that you are? The scriptures tell us to apply shraddha, an act of the Spirit of God, to life and to the Self, and to awaken to the light of the divine that we are.

KALI

Q: How can you protect yourself against feelings of anger, envy, greed, and so on, which are said to be the gates to hell?

A: It is impossible to eliminate these traits while you are identified with the sense organs. If you try to cut the head off one of these demons, another will spring up elsewhere. This is illustrated in Hindu mythology, in a story about the battle between gods and demons. After praying to Lord Shiva for a long time, Raktabija, leader of the demons, was granted a boon: from each drop of his blood that spilled to the ground another demon would spring up, identical in strength and courage. With this advantage, Raktabija went to war against the gods, and whenever he was wounded, up sprang another Raktabija. In despair, the gods went to see Lord Shiva. They found him in deep meditation and dared not disturb him, so they turned to the goddess Durga, the divine Mother, to ask for help. The goddess appeared on the battlefield and immediately took the form of the redoubtable Kali, "the Black One," with skin as dark as midnight. Her eyes were red, her teeth sharp, and her hair hung wild about her shoulders. When Raktabija saw her, for the first time in his life he felt fear. The gods went into battle and Kali stretched her tongue across the whole battlefield, thus preventing a single drop of Raktabija's blood from touching the ground. The demon was no longer able to reproduce himself and, thanks to the intervention of the divine Mother, the gods were victorious.

The story symbolizes that gods and demons coexist in us all. Depending on our upbringing, we can control our behavior up to a certain point: if we tell a lie, for example, we know it is wrong and can decide not to tell another. We can cut the head off one demon, but then what happens? Other demons appear and we may well become bad-tempered or even violent. The solution is to call on the help of Kali, who is none other than "I Am," the Infinite, in a tangible, maternal form. When you believe that the darkness in the depths of your heart is Kali, she absorbs the whole world. Even the little bird singing on the terrace is within your interiority, which is to say in Her. Everything is swallowed up by Her, because everything belongs to interiority.

When you make room in your life for Her, She shows you how to remain unimpressed by the endless definitions in the world of name and form, and reveals that all is God.

As long as you identify with name and form, as long as you believe that you are a separate individual crystallized around the concept "me," there is inevitably an egoic territory with selfish ideas and behavior. Every concept is accompanied by the desire "I want." Impatience, anger, and jealousy are therefore unavoidable. But as soon as you make room for interiority and have faith in this sacred space, in the simple form of "I Am," the presence of God ripens and transforms you, rendering all your actions good and wise. You need to maintain a certain level of practice, but the transformation is essentially effected by faith. And faith is not just reserved for when you meditate: it concerns—and should be applied to—every moment of your life.

When all concepts have been swallowed up, what is left? "I" is left, and this "I" is infinite, absolute love. It is what you are. When you realize this, all suffering connected to the world of name and form is over. You stop playing in the world of illusion and go back home.

SIN AND THE DEVIL

Q: The concept of sin plays an important part in the Catholic tradition. It is impossible to deny its existence, that there's a dark side to everyone.

A: The pair of opposites "good" and "bad" exists only in the world of name and form, which is characterized by duality. In all religions, people are called upon to do good and be good, so what drives someone, even when they have turned toward God, to do wrong? Does everyone inevitably have a dark side? Does the Devil really exist as a parallel force to God? The answer lies in the egoic territory: it is the divine Spirit that you are that gives reality to the Devil, and it is the egoic territory that, by its very nature, is the state of sin. Demonic forces take hold when a life is directed exclusively toward the outside world. Even in a life devoted to God, a residual current can still surface, a kind of inertia left over from old ways of loving and believing. The solution is to turn constantly toward God, toward the divine Father who alone is good.

The following anecdote sheds light on the subject of the forces of darkness. A man who used to attend Swami Chidananda's spiritual retreats one day started to sell drugs. Not long afterward, he began to have visions of sharp-toothed demons. Feeling that he was being possessed by evil forces, he consulted exorcists from various traditions and countries in the hope of finding a cure for his affliction. Even today, he still believes himself to be the innocent victim of demonic forces when, in fact, he was experiencing on an inner level exactly what his actions were producing in the outside world. Doesn't this remind you of Lucifer, the angel that fell from heaven?

There are innumerable levels of consciousness in the cosmic dream. The consciousness of a man who commits murder drops dramatically, and he will have difficulty regaining his previous level. To do so, he will have to face, with courage and humility, the many adversities with which life will confront him, until, after a long wait, the answer to the question "Who am I?" is finally revealed. Usually, however, such a person protests his innocence and accuses God of being unjust. But life does not make mistakes and wants only what is best for you: to restore you to what you truly are.

We must be good and do good in order to purify our hearts, but it is not enough. To know ourselves, we have to go beyond good and turn toward the Eternal, to He who transcends "good" and "bad." The Devil, or force of darkness, does not exist as an independent reality on par with God. And your nature is not sinful: it is divine, because you are the Spirit, the Immortal.

When you love God in the form of inner peace, the river of life carries you back to the Infinite. When you live with the dignity of belonging to that sacred space and practice believing that everyone and everything belongs to it, you awaken to the divine Spirit. It is a kind of rebirth. When a baby starts toddling, it wobbles, falls over, picks itself up, and, with persistence, learns to walk. In the same way, step by step, you become, as Jesus said, "Perfect, even as your Father which is in heaven is perfect."[12] You become plenitude, just as the heavenly Father is plenitude. Then all your actions reflect the divine love that you are.

DOUBT AND DESPAIR

Q: How should we deal with the way other people—family, friends, colleagues—regard our inner transformation? For example, I'm getting good results at my job, but my boss says I lack drive and ought to be more aggressive.

A: It is important to understand that the role that is yours to play in the world is included in "I Am." Look on your work as part of your spiritual life and go about it in a conscientious, straightforward manner. Be natural; there is no point trying to be someone you are not, or imitating other people. Your spiritual life is a personal matter; no one need know about your relationship with God. Be good, do good, work hard, and stick to your principles. As for the rest, look to your own business and everything will work out fine!

If your boss criticizes you for not being enthusiastic enough, why do you connect it to your spiritual life? Take a good look and see if there is not some truth in his or her remarks. Work sometimes requires absolute concentration. If I were going into hospital for an operation, for example, and the surgeon said, "Don't worry, I'll be in a state of peace and silence while I operate, and anyway you're in the hands of God!" I would immediately look for a replacement, because a surgeon needs to concentrate fully on what he is doing. However, you can be totally absorbed in your work and still be aware that God is there with your every breath. It is not a question of having to concentrate on work *and* on peace and silence: if you realize that this peace is God, which includes everyone and everything, then your job, your boss, and your colleagues are all part of that peace. Seen from this perspective, your work is God's work, an expression of His peace. Work and spiritual awakening are not contradictory—indeed, they can converge and lead you to the Infinite. Believing that there is work on the one hand and a spiritual path on the other is to look at things from the wrong angle; there is no separation between the two.

As far as your family is concerned, it is normal that the changes you are undergoing might seem suspicious. "What's happened to her? She has stopped eating meat and doesn't drink anymore. She's no longer interested in gossip and in the morning she sits in a corner meditating in front of a photo. It's weird—let's just hope she's not got caught up in some cult!" At some point, you are going to be crucified by your family and friends, and this is part of the path. Nevertheless, they too, exactly as they are, are part of that peace and silence. It is up to you to decide whether you want to go back and get caught up in the dream so as to keep them happy, or whether you want to return to the Infinite and awaken to the Eternal. The world is full of ways of thinking and doing that we are expected to follow like sheep. "You don't drink? You don't smoke? Then you're no friend of mine!"

Here is a story that illustrates this well. Ten people were in the hospital after an eye operation. They were all in one room and the doctor said to them, "Listen carefully: it is extremely important that you remain lying down, because if you sit up you'll become permanently blind. Do as I say, it's essential for your recovery."

The ten people went to sleep. Unfortunately, in the middle of the night the patient at the end of the row had a nightmare. He woke with a start and found himself sitting up.

"Oh, no!" he thought. "The doctor told us to stay lying down and now I'm going to go blind!" His eyesight was fading but he could still see the man on his left lying fast asleep. "It's not fair!" he thought, and a wave of revolt rose up in him. He leaned over and shook his neighbor, "Hey, wake up! Guess what's happened!"

"What?" said the neighbor, sitting up in terror. "What's going on?"

"I just had a terrible nightmare," said the first man.

"So what, why should I care?" said his neighbor, who suddenly realized that he was sitting up and would become blind. Rage surged up in him. "I don't believe it, I must be dreaming!" And seeing the man on his left lying fast asleep, he leaned over . . . and so on down the line!

If you have never given your friends and family any cause for concern, why shouldn't they trust you now? It is ironic that some parents are prepared to let their children sail solo around the world because it is the sort of adventure that corresponds with the norms of society today, but they regard a journey into the inner self as dangerous. I am not denying that there are people who take advantage of others, cults undoubtedly exist, as do deviants; but couldn't your friends and family give you the benefit of the doubt where your decision to turn toward God is concerned? Jesus said, "For whosoever shall do the will of my Father which is in heaven, the same is my brother, and sister, and mother."[13] So what is new?

Q: And despair?

A: Despair is a bottomless pit. It comes from identifying with body and mind, which creates a feeling of separateness from the "all." When a wave identifies with its form, it thinks it is separate from the ocean. The light that you are, which on the human plane is your power of loving and believing, is invested in the images of the world and believes they are the truth. Sooner or later, this apparent truth is shown to be false, at which point the wave feels its world wavering, nothing firm to hold on to. It experiences the infinity of the ocean as monotony and loneliness and turns to noise and activity as a distraction to help push these painful feelings under the carpet. It thinks it will find happiness in the material world but it never can, and this opens the way to despair.

Sadness, boredom, and despair are masks worn by the Infinite in order to call you back home, to where you are bliss. The cure for these painful feelings is to answer the call. For the sages and for us, making God the purpose of life has proved the best remedy.

PEACE AND NOSTALGIA

Q: At times peace feels like nostalgia or sadness. When I'm in peace, I sometimes go from feeling elated to feeling sad, as though, where the Absolute is concerned, there was something missing, and this is painful.

A: Your sense of being an individual is slowly but surely dissolving; it is nevertheless still present in a residual form and it is this that experiences interiority as sadness or boredom. On the spiritual path, there is a horizontal plane where the work of dissolving concepts in the water of "I Am" takes place. There is also a vertical plane where you awaken to the divine Spirit, which rises like the morning sun when you live with the conviction "My Father and I are one and one alone."

True joy comes into your life only with the Spirit. Many people feel happy without realizing the source, but on the spiritual path we make a conscious effort to awaken to the source, whose very nature is joy. Remember that life has one purpose only. When you live with the conviction that you are one with God, even if at present you do not know where or how, if you have faith that He will reveal Himself to you in this lifetime, then a feeling of fullness and bliss arises that greatly diminishes your suffering. On the human plane, there are many things to enjoy that also help diminish sadness. All you need to do is use the precious gift you were given at birth: the power of thought. Contemplate nature while cultivating thoughts of God; be happy contemplating the eternity that awaits you; rejoice in His presence. Be happy!

Q: So suffering only disappears when you awaken to the divine Self?

A: Knowledge is made up of three parts: acquiring knowledge, putting it into practice, and sharing it with others. When you are cooking, for example, you begin with a theoretical knowledge of the recipe. You then go to the kitchen to prepare the dish, which is already more fun. But the best moment of all is when you take the food to the table and share it with your family or friends. Your enjoyment increases at each stage.

In the same way, the highest knowledge is, "I am one with the divine Spirit." You are now aware of this and that is good. But there is more. Put this knowledge into practice by setting aside certain times of the day for "being" the Spirit. This is done by the act of believing that it is what you are.

Gradually, the Spirit awakens and the plenitude that is then revealed begins to free you from unhappiness. The best part comes last: where you are Spirit is the love of the Father, the infinite love that you are and to which you bear witness through your actions. That is where the greatest joy lies.

Q: If I've understood correctly, all my problems come from a mistaken understanding of myself; so if I've been wrong all these years, I might as well just shoot myself! I feel despair.

A: Shoot yourself? What an idea! Perhaps you started out late on the path?

Q: It makes me furious when I hear that. In fact, I started out when I was in my twenties.

A: And you gave up?

Q: No!

A: So what's the problem?

Q: I can't get there! "It" doesn't happen.

A: First of all, there is no point being furious. When you were in your twenties, you no doubt wanted God, but then your house, family, work, and many other things began to compete with your desire for God. You say "it" doesn't happen, as if there were a God outside you whom you expect to do the job for you. At the moment of death, most people who have lived disconnected from inner life experience the burning regret—even if they do not always express it openly—that they have not achieved that for which they were given a human birth,. Do you know why? Because the divine Spirit that you are knows at every step that human life has one purpose only: to walk toward God and go back home. You have put this goal aside for most of your life, and now you are furious because the years have gone by and yet and yet.... Whose fault is that?

But it is never too late to walk toward God and go back home. The efforts you made to seek God are not wasted and count in your favor. People remain trapped in the dream for so long that it is often the years ahead that are important and not the time lost.

You are familiar with the path and the various aspects of the practice. All you need to do is make God your sole purpose and the river of life will inexorably carry you back to your true home. The wave that has been churning for so long must now settle into the current that flows back home.

Q: And leave everyone else behind?

A: Because you think that everyone else is in your hands? Do you really believe that you can take people with you by remaining with them? You don't leave anyone behind! When you love God in the form of peace and silence, there are no "other people." In this peace, we are all one.

Q: I can take others into this peace and silence, but not myself.

A: What do you teach? What beliefs do you share with your students?

Q: That they are worthy of love, that they have love inside them, that they are one with God—although I don't necessarily express it that way. But the problem is that I can't apply it to myself!

A: My advice is to apply it to yourself before trying to share it. Students cannot go further than the instructions given by their teacher, and people who give spiritual teaching without having had a profound experience remain trapped at the level of the teaching they dispense.

Your anger and revolt come from the burden you carry because you think you are responsible for people who belong not to you but to God. There is humility in the attitude "not in my hands but in Thine," a lack of desire to control, and this is essential when you teach. The true teaching that leads to awakening to the divine Self can only be undertaken by someone who has received a direct commandment from God.

THE DEVIL'S FAVORITE INSTRUMENTS

One day, the Devil decided to hold a sale. He set up a stall with many colorful and well-polished instruments, each more attractive than the next. Jealousy was priced at $10,000, avarice at $15,000, and hate at $30,000. But at the end of the counter were two old and ugly instruments, all rusty and covered in dust. One carried a $1,000,000,000 price tag and the other a $2,000,000,000 tag.

Curious about this, a friend of the Devil said, "Hey, Devil, why are you charging so much for these instruments? No one is going to buy them!"

"Listen, my friend," said the Devil with a grin, "those are my two most valuable instruments. They allow me to control all the others and replicate them whenever I like! Better still, no one knows they're mine."

"Really?" said the friend, intrigued. "And what are they?"

"I'll tell you, because you're my friend," said the Devil, "but you must never tell anyone else. They are doubt and despair."

On the path of awakening to the Spirit, "a time in the desert" is almost always inevitable, like the years Moses spent in the desert before he reached the holy mountain. But if you have made God the supreme purpose of your life, know that you can go forward with complete confidence. With patience and perseverance, you will reach the goal in this lifetime. The only obstacles that can prevent you, or make you lose ground, are doubt and despair.

Progress also depends on your awareness and strength of aspiration. At one spiritual retreat a woman said to Swami Chidananda, "Swamiji, I've been coming on retreats now for thirty years and I still haven't realized God! Why?" "It's true that you have been coming for thirty years," Swamiji replied, "and there's no doubt that you want God. But you have also clung to the idea of 'my' children, 'my' house, and 'my' car."

In deep sleep, none of these exists and yet you are content. Abide in His presence with complete trust, like a child in its mother's arms. When you have ripened in His presence, the sacred state of deep sleep reveals itself to you in the waking state and frees you from all doubt and fear. In this inexpressible state, you realize that you are That.

4.

ACTIONS

THE ROOT OF ALL PROBLEMS

The Bhagavad Gita invites us to live each breath with the attitude "It is not I who am doing, but Thee," which means offering all our actions spontaneously to God. This makes you more aware, more efficient, and more alive to the present moment. In their ignorance, the people who think they are in control of their lives, who are sure they know best, misinterpret this as an invitation to sit back and do nothing. Big mistake! When you adopt the attitude "not I but Thee," the breath of life flows through you, carrying out its work in the world while revealing to you the plenitude that you are.

A story goes that many years ago at a religious festival in India, a king provided food for more than forty thousand people. In those days the prestige of a ruler was measured by the number of poor he could feed, so the king thought to himself, "Not bad! No other king around here has managed to do what I have done. I've achieved something truly great!" In those days, kings also had spiritual guides to lead them to the truth and keep them on the path of righteousness and duty. Like any other disciple, a king, however rich and powerful, held his master in deep respect. This king's spiritual guide was the great sage Vishwametra, who, when he got wind of his disciple's outburst of pride, strode off to the palace to find him. Ignoring the marks of respect he received on the way, the sage went straight to the royal quarters and addressed the king severely, telling him to fetch his sword and follow him outside. The king promptly obeyed. The two men went to the garden and stopped in front of a rock. "Split this rock in two," ordered the sage. The king did as he was told, and out of the rock sprang a toad, which immediately jumped into a nearby pond. "Now," said the sage, "tell me, who looked after the toad when it was inside the rock?"

And let me ask you this: What makes you heart beat? What makes your eyes see? What enables you to think, feel, or remember? Is it your human form, which is what you believe you are? No, it is life itself! These faculties can disappear at any moment, and will inevitably disappear when the body dies. They are wonderful gifts that are on loan to you—it is up to you to put them to good use.

THE GREATEST SERVICE

Our minds have a strong tendency to want to "save humanity." "Why don't they do it the way we do?" "How can they leave all those poor people and not take care of them?" and so on. Service can take many forms, but one of the greatest services you can render humanity is to mind your own business!

On one of my airplane journeys, I got into discussion with a German who started criticizing the Indian public services. It was soon after German reunification and I said to the man, "In West Germany, with a population of some sixty million people, you complained when you had to spend €300 billion to raise the standard of living of some sixty million East Germans to the level of the West. Imagine what would have happened if your population had been the same as India's! But as you may have noticed, that democracy of a billion people isn't doing too badly." This may have given the man food for thought, because as we left the airplane he came over and thanked me.

Until you know how to put yourself into other people's shoes, it is better not to criticize.

YOU CANNOT HELP ANYONE

Human life has been given to us to realize God, not to save the world. If you are on an airplane and the cabin pressure drops, you are asked to place the oxygen mask over your own face before helping children with theirs. It is the same in spiritual life. You cannot help anyone, because true help comes from the principle that has looked after the universe for all eternity; it cared for us before our birth, cares for us during our lifetime, and will care for us after our death. It is God who helps. He gives us the opportunity to become His instrument, and the fruits of our actions are His. A doctor can sew up a wound, but the power of healing is not in his hands.

Q: But isn't service part of sadhana?

A: Of course. But there are two kinds of service. The following story illustrates this point. There was once a rich and famous woman who lived in the same building as a simple man. The rich woman was the ambassador for a big humanitarian organization and part of her job was to arrange fund-raising parties for influential people. From time to time she made visits to developing countries, where she was photographed for gossip pages of magazines. She regarded herself as some kind of savior, "a person who helped and got things done," and this gave meaning to her life.

The simple man was married, with three children. He worked in the city and because of traffic had to leave home at seven in the morning so as to be at his desk by nine. He rose every morning at five and spent an hour in communion with "I Am." The divine love that was awakening in him made him attentive to his family, whose lives as a result were paradise on earth. The quality of the time the family spent together was more important than the quantity. On his way to work, the man enjoyed recognizing that other passengers on the bus belonged to God in the form of "I Am." A smile here, a kind gesture there, flowed naturally from this attitude and everyone he met was touched by it. He was always aware of any opportunity to serve. He immediately gave up his seat to an elderly person or a pregnant woman. When he saw a beggar in the street he gave him money, because in his interiority he acknowledged the beggar as a brother. At the office, his attitude was, "It is not I who am doing, but 'I Am.'" In this way, he remained permanently connected to the principle that looks after everything, as if connected to an electrical current. When he sometimes forgot to keep up this attitude, he did not fret but thought to himself, "If God decides to manifest as forgetfulness, who am I to make a fuss?" He was not rich and could not give away much money. He was in a similar situation to most people.

In the same building as the rich woman and the simple man lived an old lady who received few visitors. One evening, the old lady was feeling particularly lonely. The rich woman came home, walked straight past the old lady's door and up to her apartment. But when the simple man came home, some power stopped him in his tracks and made him turn gently toward the old lady's door. He went in and they spent a few minutes talking together. This lit up the old lady's whole evening—and the following days too because she became like a grandmother to the man's children.

The rich woman did good works, but because she had not made room in her life for interiority, she remained in the world of name and form, which is death.

EMOTION AND COMPASSION

Q: You've said that people who suffer are in the hands of God and that it's not our job to look after them.

A: No, I never said that!

Q: I thought I understood that we mustn't interfere, that it's not up to us to save people; that it's up to God?

A: What I said is that you have the opportunity to serve but not the power to help. This is a common misconception. You see "others" suffer—what "others"? Our sense of individuality is part of the water of life and at that level there is no separation. Every name and form is an expression of "I Am," in which all the suffering of the world is contained. When you see someone suffering, you see "another person," but for me that person and their suffering are here, in God in the form of "I Am." You feel separate from God, but for me God is here, in the form of "I Am." He is not separate. The nature of the egoic territory is emotion and commotion. My nature, in the form of "I Am," is service and compassion. At the Divine Life Society we have a free pharmacy as well as a general hospital. We also run a hospital for serious cases of AIDS, tuberculosis, leprosy, etc. We take in rape victims and anyone who has been abandoned—even stray dogs.

Q: But if it's our children who are suffering, we can't help feeling responsible.

A: The suffering of children must be seen from the same perspective; there is what you can do and what you cannot. Your children's lives are not in your hands. Children are dependent on you for a while and the service you render to them during that period is a loan made to you for a limited time. Then the chicks spread their wings and your influence and presence diminish. The presence of God, however, is there at every moment of their lives, whether they are aware of it or not. As for your responsibility toward your children, it is linked to your attitude as a parent. When you see you have made a mistake, you need to acknowledge it and change your behavior accordingly. When your attitude is to bring the presence of God into your actions, He guides your steps and everything usually turns out fine!

"LOVE THY NEIGHBOR AS THYSELF"

Q: Shouldn't we care about other people's suffering? Do we just forget about it?

A: You must first change your perception of suffering by ceasing to believe in the idea of being a person separate from other people. This is the main cause of suffering. It is the individual you think you are, defined by name and form, who suffers. Just as on an airplane you have to put your oxygen mask on first before helping children with theirs—if you lose consciousness, you are no help to anyone—so you must first address your own suffering, while recognizing the divine nature of interiority.

Q: But there is so much suffering, all these wars. . . .

A: Are you in a position to make a real change in the suffering of the world, or do you hope that your thoughts will arouse people's consciences? Are you going to do something about it yourself or will you leave it to "others"? It is difficult enough to get your own children to do what you want! What sort of influence do you think you can have on the world? You cannot solve anything while you remain trapped in the concept of being an individual who sees "other people" suffering. "Other people's" suffering is part of your interiority and that is the key. You have to renounce the idea of being a separate person, and the notion of "others" has to disappear. There are no "others," we are all one. It is far more useful, for the good of everyone, to learn to see the world through God's eyes.

The commandment "Love thy neighbor as thyself" is not addressed to the individual you believe yourself to be, but to the reality in you, to "I Am." You cannot love your neighbor as yourself while believing yourself to be a person. You can try, it is highly laudable, but it is impossible to put into practice because it is the mind and intellect that will be trying to love, and they are subject to the laws of attraction and repulsion that govern the world. The commandment, however, implies totality. My nature, in the form of "I Am," which is identical to yours, does one thing only and that is to serve.

The world is evolving all the time on many different planes and does not depend on you or me. Many people have a long road ahead of them before they decide to go back home—just as we did at a certain point in our evolution. God has given us the privilege of being able to serve His children. As far as the rest is concerned, it is He and He alone who is in charge here. Let Him look after His business!

KARMA AND HUMANITARIAN AID

Q: I'm a little confused. I understand the notion of karma, which accounts for what happens to us in life—when a woman loses her husband in an accident or earthquake, for example. I also understand that everything is contained in interiority, which is Mā, and that God does everything, but I can't put the two together. If it's written that the woman must lose her husband and undergo that experience, aren't we getting in the way of karma if we try to help?

A: Everything happens according to the divine plan. What makes you think that helping the woman takes place outside His law? You have misunderstood the meaning of "Mā does everything" and think that all you have to do is sit back and wait for things to happen. But Mā is just as much action as contemplation. When you live aligned with Her presence, She acts through you.

Q: How can I reconcile interiority and exteriority in my life?

A: You are trying to reconcile them with the intellect and this will be difficult until you have ripened a little at the level of interiority. Let me illustrate this with an analogy. A small apple emerges one day from its blossom and overhears two large, ripe apples discussing the sweetness of the sugar of life. Intrigued, the small apple says to the two large ones, "I don't understand what you're talking about, what is sugar? What is this sweetness? Everything seems bitter to me."

The two big apples turn to the small one and say, "Sweetness is your true nature. Don't try to understand it intellectually. All you have to do is to drink the water of life in the tree, in this way you'll ripen and your interiority will spontaneously reveal to you the nature of sugar."

Spiritual life is like the apple. It has an outer dimension, which is connected to names and forms, and an inner dimension, in which life matures while awakening you to the Spirit. Until you have reached a certain level of maturity there are some answers you cannot understand. But with time what had once seemed incomprehensible becomes clear.

ACTION WITHIN INACTION

Q: "I do nothing, everything is done by You." That's all very well, but as a human being, you have to do something—particularly if you're in a difficult field of work such as end-of-life care, when you become like a brother or sister to the person suffering and your role is to comfort them.

A: You see a contradiction between the inner and outer world. You identify with the role of comforter, which traps you at the level of your humanity. Yes, you do have a role to play, but are you that role? In the Bhagavad Gita, Lord Krishna says that we have the right to action but not to the fruits of action. You can care for someone at the end of their life, but can you get inside their head, inside their heart and their fears? Can you control what they are thinking or feeling? Do you really know what brings them comfort? Can you help the soul depart this manifested world for the nonmanifested realm?

Think carefully and meditate deeply on action within inaction. Know that the stillness you feel inside you is God. Go about your actions remembering that it is this stillness that acts and not the human being you think you are. Then the services you render at every moment of your life will be of a divine nature.

INJUSTICE

Q: I find it difficult not to react to injustice.

A: Justice and injustice are present in every sphere of life. Your thirst for justice is a strength and does you credit. But what really helps you act justly is when you recognize the one in the many, regardless of your likes and dislikes. Some injustices are obvious—theft, perjury, assault, and so on—but others are less so. If the man in front of you in a queue has not noticed that it is his turn, will you tap him on the shoulder and let him know, or will you take advantage of the situation and take his place? Injustice is present in small as well as big matters.

The scriptures state that we will be rewarded according to our deeds. We often witness terrible injustices that we cannot put right; but you can be sure that when the time comes the people responsible will be subjected to the very same injustices. As human beings, we ignore one of life's basic principles: everything we do to others we do unto ourselves. If you kill, you will be killed; if you cheat you will be cheated; if you hate a particular race, you will come back in another life as a member of that race. The more people realize that they are responsible for their actions, the more just and considerate they will be. This is a truth that should form an integral part of our education, because it determines our behavior in the world.

THE THREE RECONCILIATIONS

Q: Could you talk to us about reconciliation with God?

A: When you awaken to the divine Spirit, you are reconciled with yourself, with the world, and with God. You realize that God is not separate or different from you; He is not some big boss up in the sky while you, small and insignificant, are down here below. You recognize, as Jesus said, that "I and my Father are one and one only" and, as the scriptures of many traditions state, "Only God Is."

But this cannot be understood from the standpoint of human experience while human experience is still considered to be reality. When you awaken to the divine Spirit, you discover that the pleasures of the senses are but tiny drops of the bliss of the divine Self that you are, whose splendor and radiance are such that nothing else is worthwhile. When the world loses its reality once and for all, it is seen as the theater of the divine Spirit. Then questions such as "Why is there good and evil?" "Why birth and death?" "Why fear and suffering?" fall away, and everything is seen, in the here and now, as an expression of His perfection. But before reaching this point, people often get angry with God, with the world and themselves: "With all these wars, all this suffering and injustice going on, I can't believe in God! How could a just God allow this to happen?"

One day in Rishikesh, a man arrived completely distraught and rushed to see Swami Brahmananda, a great sage of the ashram.

"Swamiji," the man said, "a bus has just been attacked by terrorists and some poor people have been machine-gunned to death!"

Swami Brahmananda simply replied: "Everything is an expression of His perfection."

The man was shocked. "What? Aren't you horrified by such a terrible act? How can you believe in a God that allows such things to happen?"

"Perhaps," said Swami Brahmananda, "you should be reborn into the lives of these people so as to bring them a little justice. You seem to know better than God what needs to be done! Maybe you should take His place?"

Q: I don't quite understand. Yesterday you told us about a woman who came to the help of a man who was being beaten up by five other men while other people just stood around watching. Isn't there a contradiction with what you've just said?

A: There is no contradiction. But you must first understand that when Swami Brahmananda said, "Everything is perfect," he did not mean that he was indifferent to what had happened. He was emphasizing that the universe is not a separate creation from God, but a manifestation, an expression, of His essence. Since God is perfect, His expression can only be perfect. Human beings are like sparks of the divine who think they are separate from the whole. But nothing is separate. It is you, the divine Spirit, who has been playing out this melodrama in the bubble of your dream, while in reality *Only God Is.* It is you, the divine Spirit, who has identified with images of violence and destruction, and bears the consequences. It is you, the divine Spirit, who, when worn out by suffering, decides to go back home. And when you return home, you realize that you had never left, that all this was just a bad dream! I am talking to you now on the level of the Spirit. Much of the time I talk to you on the level of "I Am," which is more accessible and is the indispensable path that leads to Self-knowledge. The level of the Spirit is not accessible to the intellect and you can only really understand it the day you are awakened.

On the level of "I Am," the mainspring for action is inner peace. There is a gap, therefore, between peace and action. At the level of the Spirit, however, there is no gap, because the Spirit is action. Where you are Spirit is an ocean of infinite love, and when you have awakened to it you can but bear witness on this earth to the divine love that you are. Swami Brahmananda, whose understanding and sympathy were exemplary, was a perfect illustration of this.

Some years ago a tent burned down during a wedding ceremony in India, killing dozens of participants. That evening my master, Swami Chidananda, spoke at length about the event, about the anguish of the mother, father, and married couple, of the suffering of the family and guests. This kind of compassion is on the level of "I Am."

When I say that everything is an expression of His perfection, it is to encourage you to meditate deeply on this truth until you discover in yourself that point of being in which His perfection is revealed. Paradoxically, it is also the highest prayer.

There is no contradiction between the two levels, and they both imply, in their own way, service to your fellow human.

DAILY LIFE: RELATIONSHIPS, FAMILY, WORK

THE BROKEN BOTTLE

The problem does not lie in the senses themselves, but in the belief that they are the source of happiness. In reality, plenitude comes from the source of your being.

When I was young, I soldered the top of an empty bottle of orange juice, cut a slit in it, and used it as a piggy bank. When the bottle was almost full my brother started saying, "Break your bottle and with the money let's go buy some candy!" I always refused and went on filling the bottle. One day, I met my brother in the street. He handed me a twenty-five-cent chocolate bar and said, "Here, this is for you."

"For me?" I replied.

"Yes."

"Oh, thank you, thank you, thank you," I said, "it's so kind of you!"

He handed me a big bag of chips, saying, "This is also for you."

"For me?"

"Yes, for you!"

"Oh, you're so generous, thank you, thank you, thank you!"

He then gave me a bottle of Coke. I could not believe his generosity and showered him with more thanks. He set off up the street and, when he was some distance away, turned and shouted, "I broke your bottle! I broke your bottle!" I dropped all the precious things I had just been given and chased after him to try to retrieve what was left of my fortune.

The same happens in life. Let us take an everyday example: a man and a woman make love and think, "Oh, thank you, life, thank you, thank you!" because they are under the impression that pleasure comes from the sexual act itself. This misapprehension lies at the very basis of the universe and is the biggest trap. It is called maya, illusion. Maya takes a drop of the ocean of bliss that you are and puts it into, for example, a sexual relationship. What you do not realize is that maya has broken your bottle!

Do not misunderstand me: many sages in India were married with children and there is a time in life for that; it is natural and right. But you have received a human life and the potential to awaken to the divine Spirit, to bring the wheel of rebirth and death to an end once and for all. Being restored to your original glory is the true reason for your presence here on earth.

BRAHMACHARYA, HUMAN LOVE, AND DIVINE LOVE

Q: I've read that celibacy is necessary on the path; does that mean that young people won't have any children?

A: No, not at all! The cosmic dream, in all its beauty and diversity, is sustained by a powerful force that pervades the entire universe: procreation. Everything in the world is born, starting with the Big Bang. This force is a manifestation of "I Am," as are the circling planets, the thermonuclear reaction in the sun, volcanoes, earthquakes, storms, and, of course, sexuality.

You, the Spirit, can either shine the light that you are in the direction of "I Am," which leads to the Infinite, or in the direction of identification with the body, mind, and external world, which keeps you prisoner to the idea that happiness can be found in sensual experiences. In the latter case, you are inevitably subject to the cosmic force of sexuality. Anyone who tries to go up against this force on the human level has lost before they even begin—you might as well try to take on the tides or a volcano!

Celibacy is, however, recommended for those who follow a spiritual path. It preserves youth and memory, and develops the strong nerves necessary for the descent of the divine Spirit. Above all, it allows you to discover what in you transcends the cosmic dream and is free from the bonds of attraction and repulsion.

Is celibacy compatible with a relationship? Yes: there is a time for everything, and sexuality has its place in the life of a young couple. If they have both made God the purpose of lives, their inner world ripens and the divine Spirit gradually arises. When they reach a certain stage of maturity, desire falls away spontaneously and it is then that celibacy becomes both feasible and desirable. Initially, some effort is necessary, but the plenitude of the Spirit makes it possible and, with time, total abstinence becomes effortless because it is more enjoyable to seek fulfillment in the Spirit than through the senses. This is how "normal" development unfolds.

The whole universe, which we find so extraordinary, is but a grain of sand compared with the vastness of "I Am"—and "I Am" is but a tiny emanation of the Spirit that you are.

Happiness is not of this world. Our basic mistake is to think we can find it in a relationship with objects or people. You can have any number of sensory experiences, you can collect cars, castles, or yachts, but you will never be satisfied; on the contrary, you will be a slave to your desires. A sexual relationship between two people who love each other is natural, but to live with the illusion that it is the source of happiness keeps you at the same spiritual level until you die—and are reborn into yet another dream.

Q: Is human love just using someone else to fill a feeling of emptiness, for example?

A: No, human love is divine love refracted by identification with the human body. Although it is not disinterested, human love nevertheless possesses a spark of the divine, which gives it a certain beauty. Solitude can weigh heavily, and sharing your life with someone is both natural and necessary. Even monks do not live alone but in a community.

That said, human love is nonetheless a way of defending the egoic territory and of sweeping the intolerability of inner stillness under the carpet. And people think that they can fill this void with a spark! The "great love," the "love of my life"—all the romantic notions you find in songs, movies, and even in the most sublime poetry, all that happiness, even if you have actually experienced it, is less than a tiny drop of the bliss of the divine Self. Seen from the point of view of the Spirit, human love belongs to our primitive, animal nature.

Most of you are in a relationship, and I have never said that you cannot realize God; on the contrary, relationships are excellent training ground and if both of you are following the same path, that is ideal. You both decide to make God the purpose of your life; you repeat His name and practice His presence. His peace ripens in you and you live with the attitude "It is not I who am doing, but Thee." You acknowledge that "my" husband, "my" wife, or "my" children are not yours, but belong to God in the form of "I Am." You work on yourself so that your actions reflect the divine nature of your being. Then how could you fail to awaken to divine love in this lifetime?

Q: Is it possible, with human love, to live something noble, something totally disinterested? Is it humanly possible?

A: People make all sorts of resolutions, but to what extent do they keep them? In the first place, it is important to understand what love is. For example, from a human point of view, do you feel love toward me?

Q: Yes.

A: Try to measure that kind of love and compare it to this: turn and look inward, to your sense of soul. And if I now tell you that the peace you feel inside you is, for example, Christ, am I part of that peace or am I outside it?

Q: You're inside it.

A: Good. Now, in His peace, we are not separate: we are one. So human love, which puts me on the outside, is no longer possible, is it? And yet there is still love.

Q: Yes.

A: That love is of a divine order. When you follow the path of loving God in the form of inner peace, of recognizing that everyone and everything is contained in Him, you awaken to the Spirit, whose nature is love. Then it is no longer a question of feeling love toward the other person—you *are* love. This way of seeing things, particularly if shared by a couple, transforms family life into a paradise on earth. Do you understand the difference?

Q: Yes, you have made it very clear.

LOVING OTHERS AS MUCH AS YOU LOVE YOURSELF

In order to be able to love others as much as you love yourself you need to recognize that they are included in your interiority. When you see that your children are not separate from you, then spontaneously and without you real-izing it, they are included in your interiority, which is why you love them. The realization that others are included in interiority is the mechanism of love.

Love is human when it's contingent on attraction and repulsion; it is divine when it's all-embracing. The universal and divine nature of "I Am" is not open to dispute. You are at an advantage if you accept this, since it is what enables you to love others as much as you love yourself.

LOVE

Q: I've started practicing being in peace and silence, but I've lost that feeling of love as a warm, tender togetherness—along with all the fantasies that go with it. This has left a kind of void in my life, which makes me feel insecure. Will love come back in another form or is it there already?

A: How long do you think you can really feel close to someone in the space of twenty-four hours? Your identification with the mind and senses, which is fed by a fertile imagination, has created a "false you" that is in the habit of seeking happiness in sensory experiences. The egoic territory, the "false you," is a mysterious being with no real existence, but it does everything in this dream world and makes you think in ways that are then difficult to change.

You have given up the notion of happiness based on fantasy, and this has left you feeling insecure. This insecurity is sacred ground; it is the field of the Almighty. In it, you can learn to love the feeling of sacredness, be-cause it is your first tangible contact with God. When the Blessed Virgin appeared at Pontmain in Brittany, she said, "My Son allows Himself to be touched," just as a wave is touched by the ocean through its sense of water-ness. When this occurs, don't be frightened. The "Son" the Virgin refers to is the body of Christ, or "I Am," and you are invited, despite your feelings of insecurity, to trust Him with all your might. The symbol of this trust is the Cross: arms outspread and the attitude of I trust in You, "Not my will, but Thine, be done."[1]

What you say also calls for some careful thought about the meaning of life and the inevitability of death. Many people invest a great deal of time and money in planning for a "happy retirement"; they save up to buy a boat or a cottage in the country, for example. But when the day comes, how much time do they have left to enjoy these things? In some cases, death intervenes before they have an opportunity to take advantage of what they so carefully planned. Wouldn't it be more sensible to reflect on the meaning of life and on why we have come into this world? When you draw your last breath, do you want to be leaving the world at the same level of consciousness as you are now? It is important to dwell on this until it becomes obvious to you that the only worthwhile desire is to awaken to the truth; to go from the unreal to the real, as the ancient Indian prayer *"asato ma sad gamaya"* prescribes. This will give you the necessary willpower to stay on the path. Don't fight against your old fantasies; be happy contemplating the glory of the divine and eternity that awaits you.

Human love is selfish, biased, and limited. It is governed by the laws of attraction and repulsion: we love our own children, but other people's a little less so; one day you love, the next day you don't. Human love always lets you down in the end, sometimes intentionally, sometimes because circumstances are such that there is no choice. But happiness is a human need. Look for it in divine love, in the form of life; there is no emptiness there, on the contrary, it is *purnam,* plenitude. Find happiness in realizing that a lonely old man, an abused wife—anyone who is a victim of injustice—is also part of life. You never noticed the beggar and you do not know the ill-treated wife, and yet love is there, an immortal, unchanging love. This love does not spring from the human dimension: it is an act of the Infinite. It is this love that interests us. Fulfill your role in the world, which is to be an instrument of His peace, and let His peace awaken in you the divine love and fullness that are your birthright.

DETACHMENT

Q: Until recently, I used to be concerned about my family and friends, but now I feel more and more detached from the things that used to worry me so much. I do whatever needs to be done, but I've stepped back and now feel that I'm becoming indifferent to certain situations, which makes me feel guilty. I'm increasingly comfortable with my decisions but I no longer feel in tune with the people I'm close to. Can you help me understand what's happening?

A: To begin with, did the fact that you used to worry about your family and friends ever help? If there was a problem, if you thought they had made a wrong decision or were looking at things from the wrong angle, did you ever succeed in getting them to change their minds? Of course not, and no doubt they also told you to mind your own business! Your worries took up space in your heart because they were connected to the idea of "me, my, mine." This is why you felt as you did, in particular your sense of being responsible and having to "do something."

As you begin to love God in the form of "I Am" and recognize that the people close to you are not "yours" but God's, your inner world empties of fear and anxiety, and this can give you the impression that you are becoming detached or indifferent. It is not the case, far from it; in reality, your being is gradually being filled by the peace of God Almighty, which is an expression of infinite love that draws in all those around you. Paradoxically, what you take for detachment is the greatest service you can render to your family and friends.

You say that you are increasingly comfortable with your decisions; this is proof that the Spirit is awakening in you, enabling you to see things as they are. A distorted viewpoint is the cause of all problems in life. Your family and friends are still living in the dream world and you no longer feel in tune with them because you have understood that happiness does not lie in the external world. The only thing you lack is a little more dignity of being. You are Spirit, you are divine love; live with this conviction. When your family members tell you their problems, just be the love in their life. Listen to them carefully and understand their point of view. Don't try to change them; let them be the way they are, at their level, and love them as they are. In this way, you bear witness on earth to the love of the Father that is awakening in you. Be happy and make them happy. Divine love is the highest prayer and the greatest force for changing people's hearts.

BE HAPPY

On the spiritual path, it is important to find the point of being that keeps you connected to inner peace and awakens you to plenitude. Inner peace is the barometer of spiritual life. When you are connected there is joy, whatever the circumstances. Once you have found this point of being, your experience deepens and develops. God is plenitude, and it is natural for anyone who trusts in Him to be happy—which does not mean that you can just do any old thing in order to enjoy yourself!

Q: Doesn't being happy, in the beginning anyway, mean enjoying sensual pleasures, otherwise you might become frustrated?

A: The joy I am talking about is like the joy of a child and has nothing in common with the kind that comes from sensual pleasure. Young children are not yet crystallized in their definitions of "I Am," and yet they are happy. They live in the here and now and benefit continually from the fullness of their being. Their happiness does not come from sensual pleasure. You too once enjoyed this happiness, but you have forgotten it. Sensual pleasure drives you even further from it because sooner or later you come up against the limits of your human capacities and this produces frustration.

Q: Nevertheless, sexuality can be a preparation, an approach to ecstasy.

A: Sexuality is part of experience, a manifestation of "I Am" in all its multiplicity, but what I am talking about is to be found in the here and now, between two thoughts. To approach the plenitude of Brahman, you need a mature inner life. Sexuality draws you outward and cannot, therefore, be a path to awakening.

Q: But perhaps it's a stage at a certain level of development?

A: Sexuality has its place in a relationship, but because you are so attached to it and to the pleasure it affords you, you try to make it an end in itself. You will not find fulfillment in that direction, and sooner or later you will come up against the frustrations of age. With spiritual practice, on the other hand, you can find lasting happiness that does not depend on the external world.

DOMESTIC VIOLENCE

Q: My husband is constantly harassing me. He's violently jealous and, as the time gets closer for me to go home, I'm frightened and I'm beginning to ache all over. It's very difficult.

A: No one in the world has the right to compel you to be what he or she wants you to be, and no one has the right to humiliate or maltreat you. If you accept violence, particularly recurrent violence, it permeates you and creates a persona that you will then have to get rid of in order to regain the dignity of belonging to the divine. This takes time and involves recognizing that you belong to His peace, that you are one with God. The human standpoint in you will try to defend the ostensible security of your situation: "If I change my attitude by living with the dignity of belonging, and he decides to leave me, what will happen then? Where will I live? How will I eat?"

I am not saying that this is so in your case, but in many situations such as yours a woman chooses to remain with an abusive partner because she is financially dependent, or because she is so affected by her partner's violence that she feels paralyzed and cannot act. But, I repeat, no one in the world has the right to compel you to be what he or she wants you to be. Remember the words of Christ: "The foxes have holes, and the birds of the air have nests; but the son of man hath not where to lay his head."[2]

Live according to the words of the Bible: "Trust in the Lord with all thine heart; and lean not unto thine own understanding. In all thy ways acknowledge him, and he shall direct thy paths."[3]

Q: I thought I'd read that the highest sadhana was to bear insult and injury?

A: So it is, but there is a difference between receiving the occasional insult and being continually abused. The latter violates your dignity. It is for the love of God and the divine nature of your being that you refuse to accept such abuse. The kind of insult you receive in everyday life is very different, and this is where Swami Sivananda's instruction to bear injury and insult comes in. When you are on the receiving end of such an insult, try to focus your awareness on the current that carries you back to the Infinite and not on the current that holds you in the dream. By not reacting, by not letting yourself be drawn into someone else's dream—someone you may never even see again—you assert your dignity of belonging to the divine.

In a family context, a couple must learn to let the other be as they are, otherwise a separation is almost always inevitable. If one of the two accepts continual abuse, he or she falls into a pattern that affects their entire behavior and will be difficult to change. Everything comes down to faith and to your dignity of belonging to the divine.

ATTENTIVENESS

On a flight to Paris one day, I sat next to a man who was on the executive committee of an important bank. As I was dressed as a monk, he confided in me. He told me that none of his children wanted to follow in his footsteps because they resented the fact that he did not pay them enough attention. Although he earned a high salary, his children were not interested in his career for fear of being, like him, always absent. "How can you expect to be an attentive father," I asked him, "if you don't pay attention to . . . ," and he finished the sentence himself: ". . . Myself!" On the human plane, people often fail to see where they are going wrong, but the Spirit that you are always knows.

I gave the man the following advice: "There, deep within you," I said, "you have a sense of soul. That soul is Life. It is the principle that makes you think, breathe, and feel; it is what makes everything possible; it is God. During your working day, whenever you have a spare moment, take time to walk outside and observe what in you receives the sound of the birds singing and the wind blowing in the trees. Let nature teach you the principle 'I Am.' Flowers can teach you the beauty of 'I Am,' bees the intelligence of 'I Am,' and the sky the infinity of 'I Am.' Recognize with each breath that everyone and everything belongs to one life. Then the awareness that you are will awaken. Your children need you to be aware of them because awareness is love, awareness is Being."

Every role in life has a corresponding duty, be it that of father, mother, son, boss, neighbor, or passerby, as well as a duty to all creatures great and small and to the natural world. Does everybody really fulfill his or her duty? Remember that your first duty is to God and when that is fulfilled the others fall naturally into place.

People are often blind when it comes to duty and do not see where right action lies because their vision is clouded by an egoic territory. Why did my neighbor on the airplane not pay proper attention to his children? The answer can take many forms, but in essence the reason is always the same. Some activities absorb you to such an extent that time goes by very quickly. In this particular case, my neighbor was so absorbed in facts and figures that his inner world was completely taken up by his work. He loved his children but did not know how to enjoy being with them. He realized he was not paying them enough attention but was incapable of counterbalancing what was occupying his inner world.

Your behavior is the direct consequence of whatever occupies your mind, whatever fills your inner space. The origin of this internal "colonization" is your belief that the person you think you are is the active agent in your life. The egoic territory claims "I am the one who is doing."

Can you be active and effective without your inner space being invaded by everyday concerns? Yes, it is possible, when you recognize that it is "life that is doing." Your being is then no longer taken up with worries, emotions, successes, and failures; it becomes the body of His peace. If you practice this, peace enters your life and never leaves it. You realize that your children are part of "I Am"—proof that divine love is awakening in your life—and they will be the first to benefit. This love is the greatest force in their existence, and the quality of your relationship with them will change. Otherwise, you remain a prisoner of the petty concerns that devour your life, and under those conditions how can you see, listen, or love?

DIVINE MOTHER AND HUMAN MOTHER

Q: Ma Anandamayi said that it is important for a woman to acknowledge the "male" qualities within her. Could you tell us about this relationship?

A: It is not a question of a relationship but of a different set of qualities. There is a man within every woman and a woman within every man. "Feminine" qualities include the maternal ones of unconditional love, tenderness, compassion, patience, and endurance. "Masculine" qualities are mainly those of courage, determination, concentration, and strength. One of a mother's greatest challenges is to exercise her masculine qualities in order to counteract her deep-seated attachment to the notion of "my" son or "my" daughter. This is essential when bringing up a child. Above all, mothers need to recognize that their child is in not in their hands but in the hands of life. This requires a good deal of the masculine qualities of courage and determination. Mothers are also often trapped by fears and emotions and need to draw on their masculine qualities in order to overcome them.

Q: But emotion is also a way of opening up to others.

A: Emotion equals commotion. What is required is devotion, because it leads to liberation. Emotion is the result of the light of the divine Spirit being invested in the concept of "my" and "mine." This creates an egoic territory that, by its nature, is incapable of right actions, particularly where children are concerned.

Q: But you can simply be touched by someone.

A: Everyone is touched by the people they are close to. The question is to know what in you is touched. Is it the conscious or subconscious idea that your child is your child? In that case your relationship is restricted to this lifetime, because the relationships of people who identify with the body are located at the level of name and form, which are ephemeral. Or is it "I Am" that is touched? In that case your relationship is eternal and unchanging because, from this perspective, you and your child are one.

RIGHT ACTION

Q: When you have to make a decision, particularly where children are concerned, how do you know whether you are doing the right thing?

A: How do you know if what you are doing is right? Let me give you an illustration. The daughter of a woman who attends my retreats failed her high school exams. The daughter's relationship with her parents was not always easy and the parents decided to wait until the end of summer vacation to bring up the subject of their daughter's grades. Three weeks before the end of summer, mother and daughter were in the kitchen washing the dishes, when the daughter suddenly turned to her mother and said, her voice rising in a crescendo, "I know exactly what you and Dad are thinking! You want me to study, retake my exams, and go to college—well, I won't. *I won't!*" While her daughter was working herself up for an argument, the mother was praying inwardly, "Oh, God, what should I do? Whatever happens, please don't let me react!" At that point, she felt an expansion within her chest. She turned to her daughter and said to her calmly, "All I want you to know is that your Dad and I love you. With that, do as you wish." She went back to the dishes, wondering who on earth had spoken with such wisdom. The daughter returned to her room, took up her studies, and a few weeks later passed her exams. So the answer is: you don't know when you are doing the right thing, but God knows, so trust him in all the walks of your life.

Now don't go repeating these words to your sons or daughters. That is not the point of the story!

On the human plane, mistakes are always possible. Instead of using personal effort to try to do the right thing, bring the presence of God into all your actions and, when you make a mistake, His presence shows you where you have gone wrong and will give you the opportunity to put it right.

Human beings are conditioned to think, "I am the one who knows what to do; it's my responsibility and I won't let anyone decide for me." This is where the mistake comes in, because only the actions of the Infinite can be right actions. The question we should be asking is: "Do I believe in God?" Am I ready to risk entrusting my child to Him in a difficult situation? That is the real question!

Q: We're told that God will guide us, but God also guides everyone else.

A: The vast majority of people are not interested in following this path, and they behave as though this world were an eternal truth. Their mind is filled with all sorts of beliefs and concepts to do with the world, and their happiness depends almost exclusively on the pleasures of the world. They live disconnected from life and interiority. Yet I bow down before each one of them, because each one of them belongs to "I Am" and, sooner or later, they will return to the Infinite. In the meantime, our only job is to love them as they are. That does not mean that you should not exercise judgment; you have to decide where people stand and how far you can trust them, because the role you play in the world is also part of "I Am."

CHANGING PERSPECTIVE IN A DIFFICULT SITUATION

J. and P. are the grandparents of an eighteen-year-old woman who left home to live with them. The girl's parents never really looked after her and J. and P. were her last resort—it was her grandparents or the street. But she is a difficult young woman, unpredictable, oblivious to reproach, and impervious to reasoning. She sometimes stays out all night. Some of her friends are addicts and although she denies taking drugs, her behavior suggests otherwise. She asks her grandparents for money every day, which they refuse. They try to explain to her why but the young woman is stubborn and keeps on asking. In the end they give in so as to have some peace and quiet. They feel more exhausted by the day. There seems no way out: either the girl ends up in the street or they end up in the hospital!

The young woman's parents are mainly responsible for this state of affairs and they will one day have to suffer the same neglect they inflicted on their daughter. As for the grandparents, what can they do? In this sort of situation, you first thing you can do is work out what is possible to change and what is not. There is, however, another course. But do people ever think of taking it?

Here is a story that illustrates people's usual attitude. A king went out hunting one day with his courtiers. Spying a stag, he galloped after it and was soon parted from the rest of his company. Suddenly his horse shied, sending the king plunging headfirst into a well. Fortunately, a vine that was growing between the stones in the well broke his fall. When the king's eyes had grown accustomed to the darkness, he looked down and saw two crocodiles eying him greedily. When he looked up he saw the head of a tiger peering down, waiting for him to climb up. At that moment, two small rats began to gnaw at the tender roots of the vine that had been laid bare by his fall. His position was precarious, to say the least! He then felt some drops of liquid fall onto his face. He looked up and saw a bees' nest in a branch overhanging the well—it was honey! Forgetting the dangers that lurked on every side, the king leaned forward to get closer to the precious liquid and stretched out his tongue to catch a few drops. Alas, the honey came from a plant that was poisonous to humans.

What is the significance of the story? The rats gnawing at the vine symbolize the passage of time; the crocodiles and the tiger represent our sufferings and difficulties; the honey represents man's egoic territory and his persistent belief that happiness can be found in the outside world, which is precisely the belief that poisons life.

The story also shows that in moments of extreme distress, your one and only recourse is to bring the presence of God into your life, because only He can help you. The egoic territory says, "She is my granddaughter. I want her to be happy; I want her to study and I want her to succeed on my terms. I want, I want, I want." The egoic territory is always getting into fights that it can rarely win, thus wasting vital energy.

But you can change the way you look at your child and see that he or she is not yours but God's; and you can decide to trust God with all your heart. In a case such as this one, it might mean refusing the young woman money except when she deserves it. Your egoic territory will be crucified; you find yourself with arms outspread like on the Cross, but you are never wrong to put your trust in life. This attitude implies a certain vulnerability, which, paradoxically, leads to the revelation of the Spirit. This, to me, is the true meaning of the Resurrection. The divine Spirit that awakens in you is the highest prayer, the only one capable in a case such as this of touching the soul of the young woman and transforming her life. Following this path is the greatest service you can render to those close to you, because in the end everything happens according to the divine plan and everything is as it should be.

Every situation is unique and I am not suggesting that there is a universal solution to this kind of problem. What I do recommend is that you put your trust in God, love Him with all your heart, and live with the conviction that you are one with Him, even if you do not yet know where or how. Right action will then follow.

THE ROLE OF PARENTS

Q: You said that parents mustn't cling to the idea of "my" son or "my" daughter. What is a parent's role in bringing up children? It's never an easy relationship.

A: The foundation of a true upbringing is to acquaint children with the feeling of inner peace, with "I Am," and teach them that they have a dignity of belonging to this great reality. We have no difficulty getting them to believe in the false god of Father Christmas, so why not teach them to believe in a true God, one who will never let them down and who is present, in a simple and tangible form, in their innermost self? One day during a retreat, I took some children of about four or five onto my knee, told them to close their eyes, and asked them if they felt peace. "Yes," they all said immediately, "it's God!" At that age, children are not ready for complicated explanations, but they can learn to respect animals, insects, plants, and their environment. Their capacity for right action will develop gradually, depending on how much room they make in their lives for Life.

Studies carried out at Harvard have shown that from our very first days there is a part of the brain with a built-in connection to God. Studies have also shown that adolescents who grow up in families where God has been rejected are more likely to suffer from anger, depression, and suicidal tendencies than children brought up in families that believed in God, who have a relatively trouble-free adolescence. This suggests that we have an inherent need for an inner life, which is why parents' most important task is to help their children recognize inner peace, by sharing times of prayer with them, for example, and showing them that peace is the divine guide that is with them every moment of their lives. In this way, children follow the path of awakening to the truth, while living exactly the same sort of life outwardly as all their friends. This assumes, of course, that parents themselves have practiced dwelling in interiority, because above all children absorb the example set by their parents.

Living connected to life and recognizing that your children are not "your" children but God's does not absolve you of your duty as a parent. On the human level, you have to be there for them and meet their need for a secure, stable environment. Just as young plants require shelter and protection, children require a framework with defined limits and rules that should be applied gently and firmly. Teaching good manners and good behavior is also an integral part of a parent's role. This begins the work of dissolving children's egoic territories, and they learn that they cannot always do whatever they want, but only what is possible.

While discipline is important, it is also essential to nourish your children's individual interests and not impose your own ambitions, or use your child to try to realize your unfulfilled dreams. If you have a child who is passionate about astronomy, for example, it is your job to help him or her become an astrophysicist, if they have the ability. "But," I can hear you protest, "you have to have to be able to afford it!" Start by getting rid of your TV so as to have more time to devote to your children and see what happens!

The second commandment is, "Honor thy mother and father." Parents are their children's first spiritual guides; ideally, they are representatives of God and are the first to set them on the path that leads home to the Eternal.

CHILDREN ARE AN OPPORTUNITY FOR MOTHERS
TO GROW SPIRITUALLY

Q: You said that we should make time every day to practice sitting in peace and silence. But I have two young children, which doesn't leave me much opportunity. It's difficult, because you have to be with them and watch them constantly.

A: I once told Swami Chidananda that there was some duty I had to undertake for my mother. "It is not a duty," he said, "it is an expression of His grace." A few years later, I realized that serving my mother and regarding it as service to God was indeed the greatest grace in my life. In the same way, serving your children is serving God. Look on them as if they were the infant Jesus himself and do whatever needs to be done in His presence.

Q: But I sometimes miss having time to myself.

A: Live in His presence and there you will find all the solitude you need, even in the midst of a busy life. What is your attitude during the day?

Q: I remain in His presence, with the belief that "I Am" is doing everything.

A: That is good.

Q: It's a question of faith. I sometimes worry about not being focused when I'm in this state, and I worry that I won't be able to do all the things I have to do properly. I can't really explain it, but I have the feeling of being nowhere.

A: Inner peace is an abstract reality, and sometimes the concrete person you believe yourself to be feels lost when abiding in "I Am." But know that even when you feel lost, you are in the field of the Almighty and you are completely safe. It is a sacred realm that is more real than that which you take to be reality.

Q: It has always been drummed into me that you have to keep your feet on the ground and your head firmly on your shoulders.

A: In order to remain comfortably in this abstract reality, use a concrete concept of God and associate it with what you feel. The greatest difficulty a mother faces is wanting a spiritual life while remaining attached to her children and surroundings; wanting, in fact, to remain a person.

Q: But you have to, because of the society we live in, because of schools, and so on.

A: Attachment is a manifestation of an egoic territory. It is a conscious or sub-conscious "I want," which derives from the belief that your children are "your" children. And, because sooner or later children have to fly with their own wings, attachment is paradoxically an obstacle to their development. It is not the social environment that creates obligations but human love, created by the idea "my" son or "my" daughter.

There is obviously no question of detaching yourself at the human level, but rather of letting the experience of being a mother flow through you, as if you were being borne on a wind that carries you back to the Infinite, to where you and your children are one. The wind reveals to you the divine love that you are and where you are free. Attention, affection, play, and discipline are also important. Feeling that your children are in "I Am" does not absolve you from carrying out your duty as a parent. On the contrary, it awakens you to the divine Spirit.

SELF-SACRIFICE

Q: What is self-sacrifice in relation to love? How should it be interpreted?

A: Contrary to what most people believe, self-sacrifice is not a question of the person you think you are giving yourself to what you think the world is. It is giving your heart to God and recognizing with each breath that He does everything. This attitude is summed up in the words of the Bible, "Empty yourself and I will fill you," which invites us to get rid of all concepts, all attributes of "I Am," and let ourselves be filled by his peace.

Our minds are full of concepts: "my daughter, my son, my house, my bank account, my work, my future," and so on. Each of these concepts is connected to a further set of ideas. The concept "my daughter," for example, gives rise to all kinds of emotions—and often fears—about her health, her children, her work, her relationships. In this way, our minds become totally occupied. This creates an artificial "I" that has nothing to do with what you really are.

When you put God first, it does not mean that you stop caring about your family, on the contrary. By recognizing that God is in charge, you free them from the weight of your attachment, from your worries and your desire to control them. When you adopt this attitude, if your daughter rings up with a problem, instead of crying with her or trying to impose your own solution, you will really be able to listen. By understanding that she belongs to peace and that she is in God's hands, you will help her far more. Gradually, you will be in communion with peace just as naturally as you once identified with the idea of being a person.

FAMILY GATHERINGS

Q: You've talked about the rifts that can occur in families when one person is following a spiritual path. My desire to know God is very strong, but I often put it aside for appearance's sake.

A: Put it aside for appearance's sake? Why? Personally, if I am at a family gathering, I am happy to be with my cousins, aunts, and uncles, who are all included in this great inner peace. I am as happy as a child to be in their company! What more do you want? What more do they expect from you than for you be happy with them? But if you are there, judging them and thinking, "What a terrible noise, if only I was in peace and silence! You eat meat, do you? How disgusting! Oh no, I'm a vegetarian." If that is how you behave, you have got the wrong idea about spiritual life!

Q: I'm glad you brought up the subject, because I am a vegetarian and it does cause problems! But I can enjoy a party when I feel that people's hearts are in it.

A: Exactly! Be in the world but not of the world. Lead your life and let others lead theirs. Love them as they are. Be happy in their company and make them happy. They too are part of that great reality, so let your love and joy at being with them express itself.

Q: Because there is also the danger of closing in on yourself.

A: Indeed! You are here to be set free and not enclosed. This manifestation of the world is not in your hands; it is His expression and everyone has a role to play in this cosmic theater. When people are tired of playing, they join the current of life that carries them back home. When you were at the stage of believing that the external world was the only truth, no one could force you to join this current, so let people be as they are. It is up to life to guide them and not up to you; and if you try, you risk throwing a wrench in the works.

One of my favorite cousins, with whom I had wonderful times when we were children, boasted to me one day that he had eaten twelve lobsters. Imagine, twelve live lobsters being plunged into boiling water! What could I do? Try to persuade him to become vegetarian? Convince him to make room in his life for peace? Encourage him to walk toward reality and the Eternal? Is that my job? No! I love him as he is and I am always happy to be with him, just as he is happy to be with me.

When you are open, you radiate joy; share this joy with those close to you. There is not much more you can do but, paradoxically, it is the greatest service you can render, because in this way the peace that is ripening in you touches and helps them. It is an extremely effective prayer, the most powerful force in nature. Tornados are nothing in comparison, because all forms of nature are mere waves of His peace. Bring this peace into every aspect of your life and you will be blessed, as will all those you love.

THE RIGHT ATTITUDE

Q: When you're at work, you try to do your best to have the right attitude, but you realize that you're limited on the outside by the organization you work for and on the inside by your own shortcomings. So how do you go about doing "the right thing"?

A: If you observe yourself at work, you will notice that you are always looking for ways of improving yourself or your environment. Your first duty is to do your job to the best of your ability and to learn to appreciate the moment as it is, beyond the appearances of this world. The working environment offers an infinite variety of situations, but the purpose of life is always the same. Your divine duty is the guiding star that allows you to navigate the ups and downs of life without losing your way, and this will naturally lead you to carry out your worldly duties with increasing effectiveness.

So how should you go about your work? Live with the attitude, "It is not I who am doing but Thee; it is not I who am thinking but Thee." "Thee" here refers, of course, to God in the form of "I Am." The feeling "I am doing" traps you in the egoic territory, which is made up of a multitude of "I wants" and makes you think that something needs to be changed. Live also with an attitude of nonidentification with the physical body, mind, emotions, and opinions, and identify with the true body, with life itself, because it is life that sees, touches, smells, and thinks. Life unfolds according to His will and not yours.

You have told me that you work with drug addicts. Perhaps you harbor the idea that you can change them, that you can persuade them to give up the habit and make a difference in their lives. I am not saying this is bad, not at all; it is a good attitude to have, but good is not always best. The foundation of everything is your inner attitude. Billions of years went by before we came into the world and billions more will go by after we leave it, and yet we come into the world thinking we have to change it! Please note that I am talking about attitude, I am not saying we should sit back and do nothing. Remember that any help you give is always an opportunity offered to you by life and not a personal achievement. If you act from the idea "I am doing," you reinforce and crystallize your identification with the person you think you are. You are then more likely to make a mistake, because the exhilaration you get from feeling you can change something is liable to obscure your natural ability to see what can actually be done. Be "I Am" and know that the cinema of life unfolds according to the divine plan. This includes the role that is yours to play, in which you do what you can and not what you want.

A woman who looks after the mentally handicapped said to me recently that she had learned a great deal from her work. Learning from your surroundings is important. Instead of assuming the position of teacher, be the pupil. The "you" that then learns is the "you" of peace and silence, and your surroundings will reveal to you the joy and divine love that you are and to which you bear witness. This is the right attitude, the one that makes true help and service possible. Then when there is a possibility of changing something at work, the awareness that you are will not fail to see it, because at that moment you will be truly present.

"IT IS NOT I WHO AM DOING BUT THEE"

Q: I have an hour in the morning in which to do my practice and, if I've understood correctly, repeating my mantra will quieten my mind. But what about during the rest of the day?

A: What do you do after your practice?

Q: I go to work.

A: How do you get there? By car? On foot?

Q: No, by bicycle.

A: Well, when you are riding your bicycle, feel that everyone you see on the way is part of "I Am"; then they become like brothers and sisters. This attitude is the source of happiness because it awakens you to the plenitude that you are. What job do you do?

Q: I work as a mediator between offenders and victims.

A: When you are at work, recognize that both victim and offender have the dignity of belonging to "I Am." This does not mean that you treat them in the same way: the universality of life and your role in the world are two different things. You won't say to a man who has committed rape, "It doesn't matter, what you've done doesn't affect your dignity of belonging," nor will you say to his victim, "You must forgive him because you both belong to the same universality." It would be unthinkable to talk like that—and you would not be fulfilling your role on the human plane. But by recognizing that both victim and offender belong to life, you are able to see the situation more clearly and do your job more effectively. In this way, your work will benefit and will form part of the path that awakens you to the Spirit. You do not have to retire to a cave in the Himalayas!

Another interesting aspect is that your inner world will no longer be entirely taken up by work. When work fills your interiority, it has the effect of molding it to the shape of the people you are in contact with, which is exhausting both physically and mentally.

Q: It's true that I sometimes feel completely drained when I get home in the evening.

A: This will gradually cease when you recognize that the people you deal with belong to God. Of course, in certain situations you will still experience human emotions. There may be times, for example, when people's behavior horrifies you; but remember that these people also belong to "I Am" and that life will exact payment for their wrongdoings. It is not up to you to try to set them right or make them pay; life will take care of it. Equally, when you are with a victim who has been badly injured, who is suffering and in pain, you won't say, "Well, you deserved it!" It is not your job to talk, or even think, that way. Your duty is to see that the person and their suffering are happening here, in you, which is to say in God in the form of "I Am." In this way, you will not exhaust your energies, and your life becomes a prayer for the people you work with.

Live with the attitude, "It is not I who am doing, but Thee." Offer your actions to God and remain constantly connected to "I Am." The fruit of a life lived in this manner is to return to the house of the Father.

HATHA YOGA AND SPIRITUALITY

Q: I teach hatha yoga and I'd like to share some of your teachings with my pupils so as to take things a bit further in my classes. But I'm worried about saying too much and proselytizing. How do I strike the right balance? Is it okay to talk unreservedly about the teaching or should I hold back?

A: It is important to be clear about the limits of hatha yoga: it is a physical discipline that opens the subtle channels of the body. It leads to interiorization because it connects practitioners with their breath and helps them become aware of inner peace. From this perspective, hatha yoga is a useful aid in all sorts of activities, including spiritual practice. But hatha yoga teachers often think that interiorization confers a spiritual quality on their teaching. They forget that there is no awakening to the Spirit without recognition of the fact of God in "I Am," a step that many practitioners are unwilling to take! No act is of intrinsic spiritual value unless done with awareness of the presence of God. Teaching hatha yoga is not a spiritual instruction; it is a job like any other. One person teaches yoga, another empties garbage bins, another is an engineer. It is true that it is better to work as a doctor or nurse than as a weapons manufacturer, but the spiritual element, the divine Spirit, emerges in your work when you live with the attitude "It is not I who am doing, but Thee."

You think "I have much I want to share," but the things you want to share are mental concepts. Work on yourself before wanting to pass on what you have not yet experienced. If someone asks you a question connected to spirituality, you can answer from your own practice and experience, but you should not teach what you have not yet mastered. If you do, your pupils will be unable to progress beyond your level and you yourself will remain trapped on the spiritual level at which you teach.

Jesus said, "He that believeth in me, out of his belly shall flow rivers of living water."4 If you empty your inner world of yourself and leave room for God, then one day, on His terms and not on yours, His peace will speak to the peace in others. When this power manifests, it is unmistakable. At that point, whether you are a yoga teacher, doctor, or road sweeper, your life becomes a teaching, without you trying to share anything at the level of mind.

THE WORKPLACE: A PLACE OF LIBERATION

Q: If "He does everything," it means that He also sends me my patients. So what should I do when I'm overworked, if I want to protect my health and respect my physical limits?

A: Your working environment is what it is and you are not responsible. Just do the best you can. But be aware that your patients are part of "I Am" and not separate from you. Accept everything that comes your way as His work, the work of "I Am." This will enable you to do your job, however great the workload, while remaining fully present and aware.

Q: I understand that, but this body may fall ill.

A: The body gets tired when it acts from the idea of "my" patients. Mother Teresa had many patients but never felt she was "doing" anything. Her entire life was one of prayer. Of course, the body can become exhausted and you have to take tiredness into consideration, but it will be a different kind of tiredness if, while you work, you remain connected to the Infinite, with the attitude "It is not I who am doing, but Thee." In this way, your workplace becomes a place that leads to liberation. So there is no need to look for ways of getting away from work. This does not, however, mean that you should let yourself be exploited. Don't enter into other people's dreams. "Trade union rights" and "management demands," for example, are all part of the dream!

Work is not usually the true cause of illness, but if you do fall ill use the unexpected rest as an opportunity to abide in the attitude "God, may Your will be done," and "I am That on which illness is happening." Let yourself be blown like a sail in the wind by the breath of His grace, which reveals to you the ocean of freedom and fullness that you are.

WORK AND DYSFUNCTION

Q: What should you do when you work in a company where things are obviously not functioning properly; where some people are not assuming their responsibilities?

A: The scriptures state that whoever accomplishes their duty in life spontaneously realizes the Infinite. If your job is to put things right at work, then do so. If not, let them be. Try to transcend the narrow point of view that gives the workplace a quality of truth that it does not possess. Look at it instead from the perspective of the entire universe, in which "I Am" has transformed you from stardust to what you are today. Over and above the role that is yours to play in the world, "I Am" is in charge and not you. Let this take root in your mind. And don't think that if you change your inner attitude it will have no effect: it will be far more powerful than the superficial approach of trying to impose your will at the human level.

Q: But until it takes effect, I'm going to have to deal with a dysfunctional workplace. How do I do that?

A: By detaching yourself. The problem belongs to the Infinite, not to you, so do not make it "your" problem. Do whatever you have to do and remain inwardly connected to the Infinite. Give up the idea that, as a person, you are the active principle. Paradoxically, this allows the Infinite to come into your life as an active, transforming force.

Q: So it would be wrong to run away from the situation?

A: If you leave because things are not going your way, the situation will only follow you in order to teach you to detach yourself emotionally and to trust life. You must often have heard people complain how they always come up against the same problems, even when the circumstances of their lives have changed. Just as waves alter the shape of rocks, recurrent problems are there to make you alter your view of the world, of God, and of yourself. The world of name and form is an expression of "I Am," which is tangible in you, here and now, in the form of a feeling of peace. Communion with "I Am" reveals the great truth that you are Spirit. At the end of this process, the revealed Spirit, the "I" of your being, understands that "God Alone Is."

When Pontius Pilate asked Jesus why he had come into the world, he answered, "That I should bear witness unto the truth."[5] "What is the truth?" asked Pilate. Jesus did not answer, because truth cannot be expressed in words. Take refuge in this renunciation, in the great truth that everything belongs to God and everything is done by God. Let go of the feeling that you have to "do" something; that is what wanting God means. It is not a question of a human "I want," nor of "doing" anything, it is a question of remaining established in this renunciation and in the conviction that God is all.

PROFESSIONAL AMBITION AND WANTING GOD AND GOD ALONE

Q: The other day you asked the following question, "What do you really want in life?" To be honest, I'd say I want God, but I also want professional success. I don't think there are many other things I want, but professional ambition is very important to me. So the idea of wanting God and God alone frightens me because I think I'll have to give up ambition.

A: It is a good question. Do you have to give up professional ambition, for example, in order to want God to the exclusion of everything else? You say that the idea of giving up everything for God frightens you. You have told me the reason for your fear, but think carefully—is it the real reason? Why are you really frightened? Understand that from another perspective your work and your professional future are also part of His game. This may help you to see things more clearly.

Q: I wonder whether the reason for my fear isn't terrible anxiety about the unknown. Fear feels like a huge black hole and if I throw myself into it, I'll be completely lost. It's also the fear of dying as "me," with my name, form, and qualities, to leave room for someone I don't know.

A: Exactly! You have found the right answer. Faced with this great vastness, I remember asking myself the same question during my own sadhana and experiencing the same anxiety. It is normal. But rest assured, you will not disappear! In this great black hole, in this apparent void, are your father, mother, brother, sister, and friend, as well as your beloved. All human joys are there since God is there and He is plenitude. Enjoy the company of the best friend you have in the world in the form of "I Am"; it is not some "other" but the very substance of your being. The concept you have of yourself is an empty shell. Leave the empty shell; that is what I am asking you to give up. For the time being in your practice, overcome fear by putting the concept of a personal God into the void and letting Him comfort you. Have faith in the scriptures, in the words of the sages, and in what I am saying to you now.

THE DIGNITY OF BELONGING

Q: If someone is persecuting you or trying to harm you at work, for example, what should you do?

A: Every situation is unique and there is no universal solution, but the general rule is as follows: avoid the company of crude, offensive, unkind people; ignore the ignorant; endure the situation with patience and turn your gaze firmly to the Infinite.

That having been said, the way people treat you does carry a truth. Don't be frightened of confronting anyone who behaves aggressively toward you and saying to them, "Stop! That's enough!" You have to establish clear limits, otherwise people take advantage of you. Just because you are on a spiritual path does not mean that you have no role to play in the world. And don't forget that your role is an integral part of "I Am." You therefore have the dignity, the nobility, of belonging to the divine, which is why you must hold your head up high.

Acting from the dignity of belonging is an art. What is most important is to avoid reacting from an egoic territory and being sucked into the bubble of someone else's dream. This generates a new dream and brings you back into the world again and again. Take the opposite current, which carries you back to the Infinite.

INSULT AND INJURY

Swami Sivananda taught that bearing insult and injury was the highest spiritual practice. When someone insults you, a universal force of nature rises up from deep within you, a force comparable to that which gave birth to the universe, a powerful "I want" that sucks you into the dream of the person who insulted you. If you are completely caught up in the external world, you are incapable of seeing this force as it arises. But if you have made room in your life for "I Am," you can see it rising and decide whether to remain in the dream, with all its pitfalls, or turn to the Infinite and remain connected to inner peace, with the conviction "I and my Father are one and one only."

Q: Sometimes in my work as a therapist, my patients insult me. I've noticed that if I remain calm, however, they eventually calm down. Often they don't mean to give offense; they're just releasing their emotions.

A: It is not the same thing at all: a prison officer works in a prison but does not feel imprisoned. What you describe relates to your profession. The question is whether at other times your life flows toward the Infinite or toward the outside world.

RECONCILING THE BHAGAVAD GITA AND THE MESSAGE OF CHRIST

Q: I find it difficult to reconcile the message of the Bhagavad Gita, which says that Arjuna has to fight because it's his duty, with Christ's message to turn the other cheek.

A: There are circumstances that require you to fight. In 1939, for example, before declaring war on Germany, Britain did its best to negotiate a peace, but Hitler had already decided to take control of Europe and all negotiation was in vain. This was exactly the same situation that pitted the Pandavas against the Kauravas many years ago in India. The eldest of the Pandavas, Yudhisthira, a wise and good man, did all he could to make peace with his cousins, the Kauravas. As crown princes, Yudhisthira and his four brothers had the right to half the kingdom, but the eldest of the Kauravas, the evil Duryodhana, refused to let them have their share. To avoid war, Yudhisthira was prepared to accept just five small villages for himself and his brothers, but Duryodhana refused to concede any amount of land, even the size of a pinhead. As princes and warriors, the Pandavas' duty was to fight, so in spite of his great reluctance Yudhisthira was obliged to declare war.

Lord Krishna's teaching of the Bhagavad Gita begins just before the two armies go into battle.

The heart of the teaching can be summed up as follows: cease being the idea you have of yourself that believes it has the power to act, and become the body of life, which is truly the power that acts. God said, "Offer all your actions to me and sacrifice yourself to me." Offering your actions to God purifies your heart, and if you are established in faith in the sacred, you cease being a body of flesh and blood and become a body of life. This communion awakens you to the Infinite—this is the path of awakening in the midst of the battlefield of life.

When Jesus said to the man who had received a blow on the right cheek to turn the left cheek,[6] he was telling him to remain connected to inner peace and not to react from an egoic territory. When you are insulted, if you identify with the person you think you are, who inevitably has a strong egoic territory, the powerful urge "I want" rises inexorably and makes you want to retaliate with an eye for an eye and a tooth for a tooth.[7] But when you remain in the current of "I Am" and your prayer is, "Father, all I want is to be revealed where I am one with Thee," you do not get drawn into other people's dreams—people who, because of the nature of their egoic territories, are still at the level of insult and injury.

This does not mean that you remain passive. Look at Jesus when he said, "Woe unto you, scribes and Pharisees, hypocrites! for ye are like unto whited sepulchres, which indeed appear beautiful outward, but are within full of dead men's bones, and of all uncleanness."[8] He did not say this gently; he proclaimed it loudly. When he arrived at the temple and saw the shopkeepers and moneychangers, what did he do? He took a stick and knocked their tables to the ground.[9] If you go by appearances, Jesus might seem a violent, hot-tempered man, when in fact he was quite the opposite. So if you take his teaching literally, where is the left cheek?

Human beings have an imperfect understanding of the visible world and, therefore, of their bodies. They have the wrong idea about God, whom they reduce to a concept in their minds, and they have a mistaken understanding of "I." These three themes lie at the heart of the Bhagavad Gita, which is divided into three sections, each of which treats one of the themes.

People say, "It is my house, my land, my family, my country, my job," and so on, but the visible universe is an organic whole, a manifestation of "I Am," and just as all the waves belong to water, so all humans belong to life. The idea you have of being a person owns nothing at all.

God is not separate from you, nor is he a bearded old man living up in the sky: He is the life of your life, the sight of your sight, the subject, the object, and That which that brings these together. He is Alpha and Omega, beyond nonexistence. He is the infinite, worshipful Being that fills every point in space. He is transcendent, indescribable, eternal, unimaginable. He is That which sees all. He is Existence, Consciousness, Bliss absolute. He is Spirit.

And you are That. This adorable, unchanging Being is the "I" in your life. He is there for you in the form of "I Am," to carry you home when you have had enough of the dream here on earth.

Insult, injury, frustration, emotion, stress, attachment, love, hate, anger, envy, jealousy—all these come into our lives through our actions. When you want to realize God, the difficulty is to remain connected to inner peace at the same time as experiencing everything that your sense of "me" appears to be living through. Difficult situations arise. Imagine, for example, a policeman who discovers that his brother has committed a crime. Put yourself in his shoes: think how difficult it would be simply to carry out your duty, how it crucifies the egoic territory. Or imagine you are a surgeon and that your child needs a complicated heart operation that only you can carry out. Reflecting on these examples takes you deep into the teaching of Lord Krishna, who is an expression of the Infinite here on earth. Then perhaps you will find it easier to understand the words of Jesus, another expression of the Infinite, because there is no difference between the two.

ABIDING IN PEACE AND SILENCE IN ALL CIRCUMSTANCES

Q: How do you remain in peace and silence when you work in a hostile environment, when you feel under constant attack?

A: The more you abandon your identification with the intellect and make room for the dignity of being That, the more the nature of the Infinite, which is Consciousness, will reveal itself and free you from the situation you describe. That is the most direct answer to your question. But to arrive at this point, you need to pass through interiority, which is why I give you the advice to live each breath recognizing that the power of doing does not belong to the idea you have of yourself, but to life. Do as you do in hatha yoga when you bend forward to touch your knees or—depending on your flexibility—your toes, and then, breathing deeply, let gravity do the rest. In the same way on the spiritual plane, practice—according to your ability—the inner posture of realizing that God, the Life of your life, does everything.

Don't try to understand why the people around you behave in a hostile manner: it comes from an egoic territory that you are better off ignoring. Human beings function with concepts such as "I am a man" or "I am Spanish" and they cling to these beliefs because they find them reassuring. Identification with concepts prevents the Infinite from emerging in their lives and sustains their belief that they belong to this transitory, mortal world. It is not up to you to try to get them to behave differently.

The world is the visible expression of "I Am," and the insults and hostility you face are an opportunity for you to see God in your so-called "enemy." Live with the dignity of being That. Be happy and make others happy. Do your work diligently and people will find it more difficult to vent their frustrations on you, because insults will slide off you like water off a duck's back.

You sometimes have to go through periods when your outer life seems like a great void. These difficult times teach you that only God, in His abstract form of "I Am," never forsakes you. It is in the poverty of "I Am" that you learn to let go of your certitudes and your desire to control. Christ expressed this when he said, "The foxes have holes, and the birds of the air have nests; but the son of man hath not where to lay his head." The renunciation that consists of abiding in the simplicity of "I Am," at every moment of your life, is symbolized by the Cross.

By trusting God with all you heart, instead of relying on your own intelligence, you do not lose your ability to think or act—on the contrary!

TRUSTING GOD

Trusting God consists of seeing every situation in life, good or bad, happy or unhappy, as His expression. The role and attitude of each person depends on the stage he or she has reached on the path to the Infinite, and each person undergoes the exact consequences of their past actions.

Trusting God can be summed up by the attitude "Not my will but Thine." Say to God, "If you turn me and my family out of my house, I will not pray for money or a roof, because I trust You! I'll do everything necessary to make sure our needs are met, but I won't beg for them because I trust You! If my life, or the life of a member of my family, is in danger I will ask for nothing because I trust You! My only desire, my only prayer, is to know where I am one with You."

Experience shows, and has always shown, that when you adopt this attitude, your trust is never betrayed. Never! Because it is an absolute principle of life.

THE MAN WHO MEDITATED IN THE FOREST

Once upon a time there was a man who was determined to find God. To ensure success, he left his village and moved to a simple hut in the middle of a forest. He spent many years there, meditating and practicing austerities. One day when he was sitting in front of his hut, a crow flew overhead and spattered his head with droppings. Indignant with rage, the hermit threw such furious looks at the bird that lightning bolts seemed to shoot from his eyes. At that moment, the bird caught fire and fell in a heap of ashes at his feet. Astounded by his powers, the hermit was convinced that his practices had taken him to the height of spiritual evolution.

Toward midday, the man went as usual to beg for food in a neighboring village. He stopped at the first house, where a woman was preparing a meal for her parents.

"Mother," said the hermit, "please give me something to eat."

"Of course," said the woman, "but you'll have to wait till I've finished serving my parents. Then I'll see to you."

The hermit began to seethe. *How dare she make me wait,* he thought, *I, who have such powers?*

"Calm down, my friend," said the woman. "I'm not a crow you can reduce to ashes."

The hermit was amazed and regained his calm, as well as a little humility. *How could she possibly have known?* he wondered. When the woman brought him his food, he said, "Mother, how did you know?"

"Go to the next village," she replied, "and there you will find a butcher. Ask him."

A butcher? Our hermit nearly choked. However, after the lesson he had just received he thought it better to say nothing and set off meekly to the neighboring village. He found the butcher in the main square, hacking, chopping, and weighing great chunks of meat, which he wrapped and sold to his customers. The butcher's hands and forearms were covered in blood, fat and blood smeared his apron, and flies were buzzing about his head. Our hermit went weak at the knees and held his breath as best he could. *I'm expected to go and speak to that!* he thought. *No way! Never! As a Brahmin, I'll be defiled for the rest of my life!*

At that moment the butcher spied him. "Hey, sadhu," he cried, "you've been sent by the woman in the next village. Wait till I've finished serving my clients and then I'll come and find you."

By now the hermit's ego was completely deflated. How could the butcher have known?

When the butcher had sold all his meat, he went to find the hermit and took him back to his house. "Sit here on this bench," said the butcher. "I have to feed my parents and then I'll look after you." The hermit obeyed without a word. An hour later, the butcher returned and sat down in front of him.

"You see," he said to the hermit, "in my family we've been butchers, from father to son for several generations. I am fulfilling my dharma, my duty. I get on with what I have to do in life, while recognizing that it is not I but God who does everything. This is the austerity that I practice and it is this that has awakened me to the greatest truth."

6.

THE RELATIONSHIP
WITH A TEACHER

THE TRUE TEACHER IS "I AM"

Q: Can you explain the importance of the relationship with a teacher?

A: The path of knowledge is often compared to a razor's edge, which is why a guide is necessary. But my divine master Swami Chidananda used to say that the outer guide is but a pale reflection of the inner teacher, and that an authentic teacher never considers himself to be one. The true teacher is "I Am," which expresses its will through the divine breath that touches the heart of all those ready to receive it.

It is for this reason that Swami Sivananda said that no one should teach the path of Self-knowledge without having received a commandment from God. He himself, after seven years of rigorous austerities on the banks of the River Ganges, had a powerful experience in which Bhagavan, the Infinite, revealed Himself: "Awake Shiva!" he said. "Drink this cup of immortality and share it with all. I will give you the strength, the power, and the wisdom." From that moment, Swami Sivananda dedicated his entire life to sharing the sacred knowledge with all who wanted to hear it. The Infinite played His music through him, like Krishna on his *bansuri.*

One morning in 1997, seventeen years after setting forth on the spiritual path, I was walking through the ashram in Rishikesh when I met five young people who seemed to be lost. I asked them if they were looking for something. "Yes," they replied, "we're looking for someone to teach us to meditate." I said that as they were at the ashram of Swami Sivananda, the great sage of the Himalayas, they would have no difficulty finding someone to satisfy their desire! When they said they came from Israel, I began to chant the most sacred of all Hebrew prayers, *Shema Yisrael Adonai eloheinu Adonai echad,* "Hear, O Israel: the Lord is our God, the Lord is One." At that moment, I felt a powerful rush, like a great torrent pouring from my chest, and all five young people fell flat on their faces before me, like Moses before the burning bush. They remained prostrate, repeating, "Our guru, our guru!" Not understanding what was happening, I told them that I was not a spiritual guide and took them to see Swami Brahmananda. When I explained to Swamiji what had happened, he said, "Why are you bringing them to me? Don't you know that they have been initiated?"

I realized that the God who spoke to Moses in the form of the burning bush had expressed Himself through me in the form of that torrent, but I knew of no other example, no other instance of God manifesting in exactly that way.

When I told Swami Chidananda about my experience, he said, "You see, the Infinite cannot come to earth directly; He needs a transmitter, someone who can act as a kind of flute through which God plays His eternal music. He does His work; let Him do it and be still." And that is how I began to share the path of Self-knowledge.

Two years later, I chanced across the words of Christ inscribed at the entrance to a Christian monastery in Rishikesh: "He that believeth in me, out of his belly shall flow rivers of living water." *Ah!* I thought. *That is the key to my experience!*

The teacher is, in fact, God and God alone. When your inner self is sufficiently mature, the silence in you speaks to the silence in others, with the power to awaken them. It is the work of God that awakens God, not the work of a person speaking to another person. "I Am" in me touches "I Am" in you and, when the time is ripe, "I Am" in you will touch "I Am" in others who are ready to awaken.

This experience shows that the God of Abraham, Isaac, and Jacob who spoke to Moses *is.* I had always believed it, but such a powerful and direct experience removed any lingering doubts. The other interesting aspect of the experience was that God manifested Himself in a sacred Hindu place, at the call of a Hebrew prayer from one who loves Christ, thus signifying that all three religions are one in "I Am."

Q: Is it possible to follow the path even if you don't have daily contact with a teacher?

A: Papa Ramdas compared the relationship with that of a calf and its mother. The calf enjoys frolicking in the field with its friends until it begins to feel tired, and then it returns to its mother. It feeds, spends some time with her, and gathers strength before going back to play in the field. In the same way, you attend a spiritual retreat where His peace in me touches His peace in you. Then you go back into the world with teachings you can apply in your daily life. For a while, the feeling of peace that filled you during the retreat remains, then life on the outside catches up with you and you begin to feel the need for another dose!

Gradually the Spirit emerges in your life, whatever difficulties might be confronting you. One day I was with the sage Dandi Swami, who was over a hundred years old at the time, and I watched while two of his disciples moved large blocks of stone. I asked Dandi what they were doing. "They're waiting for the awakening of the Infinite within," he replied.

Q: But isn't it the same whether you see a teacher two or ten times, since it's the Infinite that you're meeting each time?

A: What is important is the initiation, when the "I Am" of the teacher touches the "I Am" of the disciple. This is the spark that sets fire to the forest. The rest depends on the intensity of your aspiration. If your whole life is given to that adorable silence, if you devote your entire existence to it, then what you say may be true. Swami Rama Tirtha heard a talk given by Swami Vivekananda in 1897 and was touched to the core of his being. He never saw his master again, but his burning aspiration led him to awakening. The forest may be dry, or it may still be wringing wet and need time to dry out before catching alight. The majority of people, including myself, are somewhere between these two extremes.

MY RELATIONSHIP WITH SWAMI CHIDANANDA: RECOLLECTIONS

During the six months I spent in India in 1986, I had the privilege of serving Swami Chidananda and being very close to him. At some point during the first part of my stay, I asked him, "Swamiji, you have realized God; you are one with God. For me, you know everything, so why do you behave as if you know nothing?" He looked at me and said, "I'll give you the answer at seven o' clock this evening." This filled me with excitement.

At the time, I was getting up at 2:00 a.m. every morning, doing *japa*[1] till 8:00 a.m., and going to bed at 10 p.m. At about six o' clock that evening, I started to feel sleepy and decided to take a short nap. I woke with a start: it was seven o' clock! I leapt out of bed in a panic. My room was at the top of the mountain and I ran down as fast as I could, but it took me a good ten minutes to reach Swamiji's house. I ran up the steps, burst into his room, apologized profusely, and explained why I was late. Swamiji was drinking tea. He looked at me, looked at the clock, and said, "I'll tell you later." I never asked the question again, and now, in retrospect, I understand that the answer could not have been given to me at that stage of my spiritual evolution.

When you realize God, the question and the answer no longer have any relevance. The position is paradoxical: you are awakened to That which knows everything, but you remain limited on the human plane by time and space. To a non-realized person there appears to be a separation, but there is, in fact, none.

In 1998, Swamiji invited me to spend three weeks in Uttarkashi, in the foothills of the Himalayas. In the mornings, I meditated in a small temple dedicated to Krishna. Swamiji sometimes went for a walk at half past eight, and when he came out of his room and saw me he was careful not to make any noise. I never heard him, but as he passed behind me it was as if the ocean was passing by. I did not realize it at the time, but the Infinite in him touched the Infinite in me, revealing to me where I was one with God.

Until my experience in Uttarkashi, although I had studied the scriptures for many years and knew that they declare the true Self of every human being to be the Infinite whose nature is pure Consciousness, I still lived on a spiritual plane where Swamiji was Swami Chidananda. The experience taught me that he was not Swami Chidananda, with an apparent human consciousness: he was pure Consciousness. At the same time, it revealed to me where I myself was pure Consciousness. In an authentic teacher, divine Consciousness manifests itself in the first instance as a river of peace. Then, when the disciple has sufficiently matured, it touches his or her Consciousness and reveals where he or she is divine Consciousness, just as a wave discovers that beneath the appearance of waves that there is only one Self, the ocean.

The twelve years that separated my experiences in Rishikesh and Uttarkashi were a time for ripening to the inner life by the repetition of God's name—a practice that gradually awakens man to Spirit. Swamiji compared it to the sun that rises steadily in the sky to reach its midday zenith. Initially, the intellect still plays a big part, but the Spirit knows that the intellect cannot understand that everything is That. It is when the Spirit is revealed that the true spiritual journey begins, and at that point it is no longer a question of intellect but of shraddha, the act of believing and of remaining anchored and absorbed in the Spirit.

In 1987, because of my engineering background, Swamiji sent me to meet some engineers at the University of Roorkee, to look at plans for an extension to the back of Swami Sivananda's house in Rishikesh. It was the centenary of Swami Sivananda's birth and the extension was designed to house a small museum. I had privileged access to Swamiji thanks to one of his secretaries, Ramswaroop, who was very close to him. Ramswaroop had what I thought a wild idea: he proposed to construct what was basically a six-foot-wide wardrobe room on twenty-five-foot-high suspension rods. At the ripe old age of twenty-seven, I regarded this as completely unreasonable—a point of view that Ramswaroop, needless to say, did not share. I felt I could quite legitimately insert my point of view, and when Swamiji and Ramswaroop were discussing the project one day, I interrupted them to give my opinion. Swamiji looked at me sternly and said, "I have been dealing with building at the ashram for thirty years!" From that moment on I lost my privileged access to him: Swamiji's role was to cut off the head of my egoic territory, not to encourage it.

This experience made me understand that the teaching concerns the spiritual realm and not human reason. I had reacted from an egoic territory, which by nature is quick to assert itself, and I had been crucified. The human standpoint is to think and act from the feeling, "I am right." But there is another way of being, which is to anchor yourself in inner peace and in the nobility of belonging to life, whose nature is patient, selfless, and considerate. Then when you give your opinion it springs from a standpoint of wisdom. This is the essence of renunciation. It does not mean that I was wrong about the extension, or that I should not have put forward my opinion; I had a role to play. But even when you think you are right, you must be able to listen and speak from interiority. In the end, the extension became fifteen very useful rooms and not just a wardrobe!

Many years later, I found myself in a similar situation with Swamiji and I knew that my egoic territory must not raise its head. I had a report to present to him about a matter I wanted to discuss, and the report set out a totally opposite point of view to the one he held. As soon as Swamiji brought up the subject, and before he had even asked to see it, I raised the document a couple of inches. He looked at me severely. I immediately understood and quickly put it down again.

My entire relationship with Swamiji consisted of not allowing my egoic territory to lift its head, of not reacting from identification with a concept or a quality, but from inner peace. This is painful for the egoic territory and it protests vehemently. It has to surrender the little "I." Indeed, Swamiji used to add to the last line of the prayer of St. Francis of Assisi, "It is in dying *to the small self* that we are born to eternal life."

For his seventy-fifth birthday, Swamiji invited several of us on a retreat in Mussorie. While I was there, I asked him to give me his blessing so that I might realize God in this lifetime. "Listen," he said, "there is an absolute law in life: if you want something to the exclusion of everything else, you always obtain it. As far as you are concerned, take it from me: you will receive it. But you must be patient." When I left, I felt calm and confident. A few years later, his promise was fulfilled. Because all I wanted was God, everything Swamiji gave me was for that purpose. He always placed himself at the level of a person's spiritual aspiration; he never pushed but respected our wishes.

In the bus on the way back from Mussorie, I sat next to one of the other participants, a young man of twenty (I was thirty-one at the time). I told him that it was rare to find someone so young taking part in a retreat, and I asked him what had brought him. He told me that he had been involved in an accident and had lain clinically dead for a time on the operating table.

"During those moments," he said, "I went through a tunnel and when I came out the other side I saw the dark angels of Yama, the lord of death. At that instant, a dazzling light appeared, brighter than a million suns, and the angels immediately bowed down before it. In the center of the light was Swami

Chidananda. 'You are not taking this one!' he said, and the angels immediately rose up and left."

The young man then woke on the operating table. "I didn't know Swamiji," he continued, "but when I came out of the hospital I read an article that had a photograph of him. He was giving a conference in a town close to where I live. That's how I began to follow him."

In 1993, Swamiji was invited to take part in an interfaith conference in Italy, in the town of Assisi. The previous year, my sister Ingrid, who lives in Canada, dreamed that she was in Assisi, a place she had never set foot in. In her dream there were thousands of people milling about in the streets and the whole town was in an uproar. Suddenly, St. Francis appeared in the crowd, a halo about his head. He was the peace of God on Earth and everyone was looking at him. "How I wish he would take my hands!" thought Ingrid. When St. Francis arrived in front of her, she knelt and clasped her hands in prayer. He took her hands in his and said, "Baba[2] has told me so much about you!" then placed a naked baby girl in her arms and told her to look after her. The following day, Ingrid discovered that she was pregnant, and when she gave birth some months later, it was to a little girl! Not long afterward, Ingrid found herself in Assisi at the same time as Swamiji.

On Swamiji's eightieth birthday in 1996, I too had a dream: I was sitting in meditation and he was a child, throwing his arms around my neck and kissing me, while I remained impassive. He was saying to me, "You're so lucky! You're so lucky!" I called Swamiji the next day to wish him a happy birthday and told him my dream. "Always remain that child," he said, "because even if Swami Chidananda looks to be eighty, he is, in fact, only eight. That is the secret of my relationship with God." This was the inner treasure of Swamiji's relationship with God, and his relationship with his teacher, Swami Sivananda, whose being is merged with the Infinite and who is one with the divine ocean. It is also the secret of my relationship with God and Swamiji.

When I was in Uttarkashi in 1998, I had another dream: I saw hundreds of people in long white robes, walking barefoot toward me and singing, "My God, your hand is visible." Their voices grew louder and louder until I woke up with a jolt. I had to take a deep breath. It was exactly one a.m. and I could not get back to sleep. When I recounted my dream to Swamiji, he said, in his usual manner, "Yes, that comes from God." Swami Premananda, who was in charge of the ashram, had overheard our conversation and added, "You had a dream and couldn't go back to sleep? Then your dream will come true in the next six to nine months." And indeed, six months later, people spontaneously started to arrive, without being asked, in a kind of dance that has gone on ever since. I had simply had advance warning of His plan!

This kind of phenomenon often occurred with Swami Chidananda, because he was an instrument of God's peace on earth, a saint in whose presence no one could remain untouched. He was devoid of any egoic territory, filled with holy peace and awakened to the divine Spirit; through him, God carried out His work in the world.

Swamiji was close to Mother Teresa. Not long before Mother Teresa died, my mother went to visit her in Calcutta. Before leaving, she asked Swamiji to give her his blessing. "What? You are going to see God and you ask me for my blessing!" For Swamiji, people's beliefs were not important: it was their actions that counted. Mother Teresa had emptied herself of herself and given the space to life. She is no longer with us, but as her life was given completely to God, now only God remains.

Swamiji had great humility and never made a hasty judgment. He was highly perceptive and saw good in everyone. There was an interesting link between him and St. Francis of Assisi—indeed, he was known as the St. Francis of India, a name which summed up what he represented on earth and symbolized his relationship with other human beings, whatever their race, culture, or caste.

Southern India is still very conservative. Caste plays an important role, and street sweepers are classed as Untouchables. One day, Swamiji was walking down some steps when a sweeper, who had been sweeping in front of him, stopped and brought his broom up against his chest. Swamiji asked him what he was doing. "Swamiji," the man replied, "I am just a sweeper, I don't want to dirty you!" Swamiji went up to him, took him in his arms, and said, "You see, you and I are the same. You sweep on the outside and I sweep in people's hearts."

7

AWAKENING TO THE SPIRIT

THE IMMACULATE CONCEPTION

When you live in communion with "I Am," Consciousness, which is the very nature of "I Am," gradually reveals itself without the intervention of the mind, in a realm beyond the mind's reach. As the tangible expression of the Infinite, "I Am" is the way, the guide, and the life that leads every being with infinite patience to its final destination: to the Infinite. In the Old Testament, it is called "Jerusalem," the bride of God. Hindus call her the divine Mother. She is there in you in the form of inner peace, which is simple to experience and yet limitless, inexpressible, and absolutely worshipful. She is also She who calls herself the Immaculate Conception.

Those who awaken to the Infinite in this lifetime remain nonetheless subject to the inherent limitations of the human condition. At the death of the body, however, which is what binds us to time and space, the glory of the Infinite is restored, and this is why death is a glorious moment. This is true for everyone. In India, the scriptures also declare that whoever gives birth to someone who realizes God also attains the Infinite. This was the case for Mary, mother of Jesus; she is not just Mary but the Infinite itself. This is borne out by her words to the railway worker when she appeared at the Three Fountains in Rome: "I am the one that is of the Divine Trinity."

In the Old Testament the Lord says, "I am returned unto Zion, and will dwell in the midst of Jerusalem: and Jerusalem shall be called a city of truth."

"Zion" here refers to the human body. I dwell in Jerusalem, or in "I Am," like a tortoise that draws its head and limbs into its shell. I dwell in the stillness of my being, and love and contemplate God in this form. I ripen in His stillness and, with time and patience, my inner self is filled by His peace and I am "Jerusalem." In this state of communion, the Infinite reveals itself as "I," which can only be described as "Spirit" or "Truth."

The prophets of the Old Testament set out this path many years before Jesus. When Jesus said, "I am the way, the truth, and the life: no man cometh unto the Father, but by me," he was describing a path that had long been in existence. The "I" to which he refers is obviously not Jesus as a person, but the body of peace and silence, "I Am." His statement accords perfectly with the path set out by the Hebrew prophets: it is impossible to return to the Father without going through Jerusalem, without going through "I Am."

BAPTISM BY WATER AND FIRE

Q: Could you explain what you mean by "baptism by water and baptism by fire"?

A: St. John the Baptist said, "I indeed baptize you with water, but He who is coming after me is mightier than I, whose sandals I am not worthy to carry. He will baptize you with the Holy Spirit and fire."[1]

When you abide in the water of "I Am," the mountain of attributes with which you identify no longer impress you. Factors that depend on circumstances, such as history, geography, family relationships, race, religion, work, handicaps, age, beauty, social status, wealth, and so many other ideas that human beings regard as truths, all dissolve in the nobility of belonging to "I Am." Instead of being a name and a form with a body of flesh and blood, you gradually become a body of peace and silence. This is the baptism of water, in which the first stage is to practice the presence of God and repeat His name.

Now for fire: practice accepting that "I Am" is the state of the world before creation. You are in that state, a holy state; now ask yourself "Who sees this state?" Look for the "I" in the experience. You can find it using the neti-neti technique, for example, which consists of rejecting everything that is not "I."

When you find "I," the only word that can describe it is "Spirit." "I" is in the here and now. It is where you are one with the divine Father. It is that which in you understands such statements as "All Is God" and "God Alone Is." Once you have found "I," all that remains is to be anchored in it. It is the fire that destroys the darkness of ignorance and frees you forever from fear. It is the purpose of life, and when you have found it all your actions bear witness to the truth and reveal the infinite love that you are.

It is important to abide by the instructions of the sages. Following your own spiritual path based on your own understanding leads to mistakes. When you consult a doctor, you take his advice: one medicine has to be taken in the morning on an empty stomach, another with your midday meal, and so on. In this way you regain your health. But if try to cure yourself with your own prescription, there is a strong risk that the treatment will not be effective.

RIPENING IN "I AM"

Q: The path to "I Am" seems to be one of devotion, knowledge, and service. The path from "I Am" to "I," on the other hand, appears to be more of a path of knowledge through inquiry, detachment, renunciation, and discrimination. Am I right?

A: No. What you say shows a lack of understanding. There is no real path to "I Am"; it is more a question of ripening, of maturing, because "I Am" in the form of inner peace is immediately available to you here and now. It is the life in you, and you do not need to make an effort to be aware of it. The paths you speak of—devotion, service to others, meditation, prayer, intellectual inquiry into "who am I?" and so on—purify the heart because they dissolve the concepts of "my, yours, his, hers, theirs" and make room for sacredness. But as the peace of God increasingly fills your life, it is through faith and the nobility of belonging to God that the concept of belonging to the world of name and form gradually dissolves and loses its power over you. In the words of the Bible, "Empty yourself and I will fill you."

But you are also right in that what is shared here with you here is the way of Vedanta. But even if this includes all the paths you mention, it is not through any practice you do at a human level that you arrive at your goal; it is through faith. It is faith that awakens you to truth by changing your perspective on God, the world, and yourself. It is a question of doing less, of letting go more, and of allowing yourself to be revealed to yourself.

Traditional paths are there to purify your heart, to ripen it to "I Am," but the path of knowledge requires an act of faith in the nobility of belonging to "I Am," as well as belief in the highest teaching of the scriptures: "I and my Father are one."

THE FIELD OF THE ALMIGHTY

Q: You've said several times that we have to get rid of attributes, but what attributes are you referring to?

A: They are innumerable: I am my physical characteristics, my family relationships, age, job, handicap, opinions, experience, talents, memories, my life history, my country's history, and so on. Because you have placed your belief and love in the reality of these attributes, you have superimposed them on life, which by nature is simple and universal. Every attribute has become a reference point, a prism, through which you view and judge the world. You are defined by what you judge, which is why human beings remain trapped in the external world and seek happiness where it can never be found. Every one of these attributes perishes with the death of the body; and then what is left of your children, parents, possessions, money—everything that had so preoccupied you during your lifetime?

Jesus said, "It is easier for a camel to go through the eye of a needle, than for a rich man to enter into the kingdom of God."[2] This refers not only to material wealth, but to the mountain of attributes that define the idea you have of yourself. You have mistaken these attributes for reality by associating them, to a greater or lesser degree, with "I Am." True poverty consists of disconnecting from identification with the world of name and form and connecting with God, in the simple form of your true being. Learn to live in a childlike state; let go of your usual points of reference, abandon yourself to the feeling of being lost, and discover happiness there. Place your trust in the feeling of the unknown: it is the field of the Almighty. It is His song calling you home.

Time flies by and life is short. The chance to awaken to the Spirit, to reality, is a unique opportunity, and it is also the greatest service you can render to those close to you. Nothing else is worthwhile.

Q: Is the field of the Almighty, where you feel lost when you've let go of all your attributes, a preparation for death, because at that moment you're inevitably confronted by the experience?

A: In most cases, after death you return to the state in which you were before you were born. Is it enough just to familiarize yourself with the state? Is that what the gift of life is for? Absolutely not! At the moment of death, a wave that has not made room for "I Am" experiences hiranyagarbha, the great fear, another word for "I Am." Those who have practiced meditation and are familiar with "I Am," but who have not included God in their practice, will not experience fear because they will be familiar with the state. This is good, but it is not nearly enough! When you have awakened to the Spirit and have found "I," death is a glorious moment. After wandering for so long in the cosmic dream, you regain the fullness of your being and the original glory of your true Self.

It is important to believe in God. By acknowledging His existence in your inner self, you realize that you and everyone else are one in "I Am," which is the sine qua non of awakening to divine love. The same mechanism applies to human love: loving your child presupposes that you recognize the oneness of "I Am" since all you have to do is think "my son" and the child is spontaneously included in you, and love is there. Human love, which is partial and selective, belongs to the finite world, whereas divine love is the very nature of the Infinite, and that is what you are in essence.

RENUNCIATION

Q: What are the rules of *sannyasa*?

A: Sannyasa means renunciation. But renouncing what? Contrary to what is generally believed, it is not a question of renouncing your husband, wife, children, friends, or house. You can perfectly well remain in your present surroundings and live a life of renunciation.

The story of King Janaka, who reigned over Videha and was a renowned sannyasi, illustrates this point. One day, when the town was busy preparing for the king's birthday, a man who purported to be a sage arrived at the palace and asked for an audience with the king. In those days sages were highly respected and King Janaka agreed.

When the man came before the king, he said to him, "How can you call yourself a great sage? You are married and live in a sumptuous palace, you are surrounded by dancing girls, musicians, and servants—everything that's contrary to the spirit of sannyasa!"

"I see your point," replied King Janaka, "but before giving you an answer, I would like you to do something." He called for a bowl to be filled to the brim with oil and said to the man, "Walk around the town carrying this bowl of oil without spilling a drop, then come back and find me."

The man set off with the bowl. The celebrations were at a height; all around him people were eating, dancing, singing, and laughing. Magnificently decorated elephants processed down the streets, and snake charmers and monkey trainers were drawing crowds of spectators. But our man kept his eyes riveted on the bowl of oil.

When he got back to the palace, the king said to him, "Did you see the celebrations? The elephants? The dancers? The snake charmers?"

"No," replied the man, "I saw nothing. I was watching the bowl."

"Well," said the king, "now you understand. Just as you kept your attention fixed on the bowl, I keep my attention fixed on the Infinite."

This is the true meaning of renunciation: to keep your gaze constantly turned to God.

If you think about it carefully, what remains today of the events that took place during the time of the Crusades, for example? Of course, those events paved the way for what is happening today, but what is left of the joys, tears, dramas, passions, loves, hates, hopes, and fears that made up the everyday life of those who lived at the time? Does anything tangible remain? No. In fact, the presence of an ant in your house today is more significant than anything that happened then. But the life of a St. Francis of Assisi has had an impact on the lives of millions of people and goes on doing so today. Nothing will remain of the love you invest in the world, but love invested in the peace of God leaves an everlasting impression.

VISIONS, SAMADHI, "I"

Q: Is the experience of union with God, samadhi, the result of perseverance and practice or of grace?

A: Union presupposes a state of separation, but you are never at any time separate from God. When you repeat God's name and immerse yourself in His presence, the Infinite enters your life—intermittently and without being invited—in the form of an inexpressible peace, a more or less profound state of communion called samadhi. If you look on this experience as an encouragement to continue along the path to awakening, it can be regarded as the result of His grace. But it can never, under any circumstances, be separate from you. His grace does not come and go but, like the sun, is always shining. If you keep the shutters closed, however, you will never receive any benefit. So your attitude is the key: when you have the right attitude, the grace of God comes flooding into your being.

What the Infinite desires above all is for you to go back home. Living with the conviction "I and my Father are one and one only" is the highest manifestation of His grace, and it is where you realize that His grace and you are one.

Is the experience of very deep meditation sufficient? Not really. It is an encouragement, but there is more. Remember that the goal is not simply to experience a state such as samadhi, but to awaken to That which "knows" the experience.

Q: How and why does the search for Self-knowledge begin?

A: Why do you wake up in the morning? You could say, "Because I've had enough sleep." But if you observe your experience at the moment you wake, the answer is simply because it was time to wake up. There is no precise reason. It is just the way it is. So why, at a given moment, do you, divine Spirit, decide to go back to the Father's house? Why are you here now, following the path of awakening? The answer is simply that the time has come.

Q: Is it possible to go through life without experiencing samadhi, even though you might spend much of life in communion with the Infinite?

A: Samadhi and nirvana are simply the experience of communion with "I Am," which arises with a certain level of intensity and then disappears. The highest goal is *sahaja samadhi*, or natural samadhi, which is not an experience but the "I" of your existence. When you recognize it, you realize that it has always been there; it is there at this very moment although you are not aware of it. So it is not a question of trying to attain some kind of state but of being what you are.

As for "communing with the Infinite," if you could really do this you would also be able to measure it, which is impossible. When you are in communion with "I Am," the Infinite is, of course, present, but limited in time and space by the physical body.

Can you go through life without experiencing samadhi? Experiencing the state is of minor importance, if any at all. Spiritual progress is not measured by your experience of samadhi but by your ability to remain connected to inner peace, with the attitude "It is not I who am doing, but Thee."

That said, I am not trying to deny you whatever inspires or moves you. If this notion of the Infinite helps you abide in peace, if that is what works for you, then use it.

Q: Is the practice of awareness linked to "I"?

A: That which in you is aware is an act of the Infinite. Can a person, who by definition is finite, "practice" an act of the Infinite? You can be aware, but what is that "awareness" in you? Awareness is in the here and now; it is the Eternal that you are. When you are in communion with "I Am," look for "I" and you will find That which is awareness. Your true "I" cannot be practiced or improved on. Find it and bear witness in all your actions to what you truly are.

Q: I recently read a book where several people described some powerful experiences they had had, particularly in India, which they said radically changed their lives. You seem to be teaching something else; you say that all we have to do is abide in peace and silence, and anchor ourselves in that state.

A: It is true that India can produce very powerful experiences. The French priest Father Henri Le Saux, for example, was touched to the very core of his being by Ramana Maharshi, whose gaze was turned to the Infinite but who regarded visions, miracles, and experiences, however powerful, of no importance whatsoever. India's true monuments are those rare beings who were anchored in the Infinite and who bore witness to the truth. But to attain their level, you must listen carefully to what they had to say. It is not enough to be touched or moved in order to understand how to establish yourself in what is revealed in the space of an instant.

Q: Mā Anandamayi never prostrated before anyone, because for her all was God; isn't hers an example to follow?

A: If the Holy Virgin appeared before us now, you can remain standing if you want, but you will find me prostrating at her feet! Mā was a manifestation of the Infinite on earth. Do you really think that with your current spiritual level you can see things from her point of view and act accordingly? Since you have not yet discovered who you are, is it not reasonable to assume that you have the feeling of being separate? You look at the East with Western eyes, but in the East prostration is natural: children prostrate before their parents, pupils before their teachers, and disciples before their master. For a vase to be filled, it must be emptied and placed lower than the source of the water. If you want to receive knowledge, you must first get rid of your certitudes and show some humility. That having been said, there are always ignorant people who will be drawn to personality cults and unscrupulous people ready to exploit them.

THE DREAM STATE AND THE STATE OF THE WORLD

We alternate between three states: waking, dreaming, and deep sleep. Each of these states plays a role in awakening to the Spirit. What is the role of the dream state? Analyzing what happens when you dream provides some illuminating answers to the question.

It is usually nighttime when you sleep, yet in a dream it can be daytime. In a dream there is time and space; you can meet people, hear, see, touch, eat, and smell, just as you can when you are awake. When you are dreaming, the dream world seems very real and you believe that you are an individual experiencing the events in your dream. You are the subject and there is a world of objects out there that appears to be separate from you. The law of cause and effect seems to operate: if, for example, you dream that you drop a bottle, you think you are responsible for the bottle falling to the ground. You believe that you have free will and that it is you who decides when to get up and go out, when to talk and when to be quiet. Then the alarm goes off and you wake up.

The first thing to notice is that the dream world and everything in it, which had seemed separate from you when you were asleep, was, in fact, inside you. You were mistaken in thinking that your surroundings were outside you and you realize that the person you thought you were in your dream was not real. You are not that person and yet you believed it. When you analyze the dream state, the law of cause and effect that had seemed to operate was, in fact, absent. If you drop a bottle in your dream, are you really responsible for it falling to the ground?

In a dream, you think you have free will, but when you wake up you realize there was no such thing. The dream unfolded as it had to unfold, just like in a movie. Your mistake was to identify with the person you thought you were in the dream and to believe that you were in control of your fate. When you wake up, you realize that you are not that person, so the question of free will no longer arises and is no longer relevant.

The person you thought you were in your dream is identical to the person you think you are at the moment. You have no difficulty admitting that you are not the person in your dream, so isn't it logical to conclude that you are not the person you think you are in this so-called waking state?

If the dream state was the only state that existed, how could we distinguish it from the waking state? You could spend your whole life searching for the truth, but you would be trapped in the dream and you would never understand what was really going on. This is why we need to recognize that the dream state is an expression of the grace of God, because it provides us with a different perspective on the waking state and, as we ripen in "I Am" and the Spirit awakens, it sheds a different light on the perception we have of ourselves and the world.

Q: But there are people out there who are hungry—that isn't a dream!
A: Who is suffering? Who is hungry when you are hungry? When you are in the dream state, which you mistake for the waking state, and you feel hungry, your suffering is real. But until you try to find the answer to the question "Who am I?" you will never understand the true nature of the world. The answer to the question is that you are Spirit, and where you are, there the Infinite is. There is no death or suffering there, no desire or need; on the contrary, there is absolute fullness of being, absolute consciousness, and

absolute knowledge. You are That. The role of suffering is to arouse in us the burning desire to leave the dream and go back home, and this forces us to turn our gaze to God.

All suffering is a manifestation of life, just as waves are a manifestation of water. When you see the suffering of others through the eyes of "I Am," you realize that the true nature of "I Am" is prayer and compassion.

Bear in mind that as long as you remain trapped in the dream, you are subject to the law of cause and effect. Recently, a government wanted to put a stop to any further immigration and ordered its army to tow onto the high seas a boatload of refugees who were within two days of landing on its shores. As the vessel had neither engine nor sails, its occupants were condemned to a slow and painful death. The people responsible for this will live out their lives more or less normally. After death, and after a certain lapse of time, they will come back to earth and find themselves in the same situation as the refugees, and they will have to endure the same terrible suffering. In other words, they will experience the exact same suffering that they had inflicted, because on the level of the world that is a law. When you see suffering, you see only its effect, but you also need to look at the cause, because life does not make mistakes.

Q: Yesterday I went to Rishikesh and ever since I've been haunted by the image of a tiny, stick-thin woman holding her child. Usually, I'm happy to give to beggars, but I turned my back on this woman because she clung on to me so hard, I couldn't bear it! Now I can't get the image of her out of my mind, particularly as it was near the slum area along the Ganges.

A: What you describe is your perception shaped by a human emotion. Emotion creates commotion, but what we are looking for is devotion. Emotion comes from your identification with the human person and its notions of justice and goodness. You think that your happiness is greater than the beggar woman's, but when she is happy, her joy is no different from yours. If you want to act justly, begin by loving God in the form of His peace, because the whole universe is His and the beggar woman is in His hands. When someone understands this, what happens? Joy and love arise. So even if the person lives in extreme poverty, he or she is richer and happier than you.

Q: That's hard!

A: I repeat: everything you undergo in this world is exactly what you deserve. There are no accidents. The universe, in its apparent chaos, is, in fact, perfect. Everything is in its place, and the way you live, love, and believe prepares the scenario of your next dream—the next cinema—down to the last detail.

Q: You say that all my actions are preparing the next cinema. Does God make movies, is he behind the camera?

A: He is the producer, director, actor, screen, projector, audience. . . .

Q: So it's up to us to try not to remain in the movie?

A: Yes, it is up to you to decide whether or not you remain trapped in the movie. When you are tired of suffering, you say, "I've had enough, I'm going home!"

Q: But what's the point of all this cinema?

A: What makes you think it ever happened? You could also ask why, how, and when all this began, but because you are asking the question from within the movie, you cannot find the answer. You can ask yourself in a dream when the dream began, but when you wake up you realize that the events in the dream never happened, so the question does not arise. This so-called waking state is just one long dream and you are not the person you think you are. Find out who is asking the question. Find the "I," and for the transcendent being that you are, all these questions will fall away of their own accord.

YOGA-NIDRA

Of the three states we experience in life, deep sleep is the most important. When your mind is sufficiently purified and you have ripened in "I Am," the time comes when you can recognize the state of deep sleep in the waking state. When "I" is revealed in this state, the only word that can describe it is "Spirit," and the ultimate purpose of human life is realized.

In deep sleep you are unaware of both the existence and the absence of the world. There are no thoughts, feelings, or memories—there is, in fact, no experience whatsoever; there is nothing at all. You are still there, but disconnected from all physical and mental activity. The existence of the world and the entire sum of your experiences are erased; not even the most terrible suffering can affect you. And yet you have not disappeared, since you can get up in the morning and say, "I slept well." Something in your sleep "knows" you have slept well.

How do you recognize the state of deep sleep in the waking state? Tell yourself that it is, for example, two o'clock in the morning and that you are fast asleep. The state of deep sleep then arises in your waking consciousness. This is true *yoga-nidra,* which has nothing to do with yoga-nidra as practiced in yoga classes. True yoga-nidra is an *upadesa* of the Upanishads, an instruction given by a qualified guide to a pupil who has ripened sufficiently in "I Am" to recognize the state of deep sleep in the waking state. This fourth state is known as ishvara or *turiya.* The point of the practice is that the Consciousness that sees the state of deep sleep is not human consciousness distorted by the ego, but the divine Consciousness that you are. It is the divine Spirit.

The "I" can reveal itself on the human level and on the level of "I Am," but this is not sufficient. People can have a powerful spiritual experience in which there is euphoria and the realization that all is God, but after a while the experience disappears. It is only when the state of deep sleep is recognized in the waking state that the "I" is Spirit and not some transient experience. The path to the fourth state is extremely precise; it consists of several stages and no one should embark on it without a qualified guide.

However, before arriving at this state, the state of deep sleep can serve as a reference point to help you remain connected to inner peace whenever your mind is disturbed or you feel overwhelmed by emotion.

FREEDOM

Your true being is absolutely free. But here, on the human plane, you are only as free as the rules and regulations allow you to be. Your freedom is conditional. For example, you have to produce proof of identity when you travel. When you are driving, you have to respect the rules of the road. If you want to teach, however much knowledge and experience you might possess, you still need a diploma. If you are a foreigner, you need a work permit. When you require medical attention, you have to consult a doctor registered in the country where you live; a doctor friend from another country who happens to be visiting cannot give you a prescription. The list is endless. I am not in any way criticizing the merits of these regulations; I am merely pointing out the limits to the freedom you think you have.

Then there is the consumer society—aren't all the images of the so-called happiness that it promotes a form of tyranny that enslaves people? Yet the main factors that inhibit free will are the three *gunas,* the forces of attraction and repulsion inherent in nature. Two people with the same egoic territory, living in an identical environment, will act in exactly the same way because they have no freedom in relation to these forces. Their actions are as predictable as those of animals in the wild. This is the rule for anyone who lives on the level of the egoic territory. And, however outrageous it may seem, the intellect—even in its most subtle and refined form, such as in poetry, art, or music—does not enable you to escape this law.

And yet you are "Freedom." But this freedom, because it is the very nature of the Infinite, cannot be found in the finite world. It is not accessible to the human person, to the idea you have of yourself. It is to be found there where "I" is, and the only word that can describe it is Spirit. There, all barriers fall. There, you are free. In the words of the great sage of the Himalayas, Swami Sivananda: "Know thyself and be free."

"THIS BODY IS A PRISON"

I was talking about God-realization one day with a brother monk at the ashram in Rishikesh. Using the metaphor of water and the ocean, I said that realizing God could be compared to a wave that has discovered the "I" of its "water-ness" and abides in its lifetime where it is one with the ocean. The vastness of the ocean cannot, however, give itself fully to the wave, because a wave is limited in time and space by form. It is only at the moment of death that the wave receives its full "oceanity." It is a glorious moment, because the wave then returns to its true home. In the same way, realized beings, having discovered "I" and dwelled throughout their lives where they are one with the Infinite, upon death receive the glory of the Father and return to His house. This is the great revelation, the end of the cycle of death and rebirth. It is the true meaning of the word "Apocalypse."[3] *Sarvam brahmamayam,* everything is Brahman, all is the Absolute.

My brother monk was not convinced by this explanation, so I said I would ask our sainted master, Swami Chidananda. Swamiji was in bed, aged ninety-one, and a few months away from leaving his body. "Swamiji," I said, "as I understand it, for those who have realized God and who have remained anchored in the Self throughout life, the moment of death is a glorious moment, because the Infinite is restored to them."

Swami Padmanabhananda, another brother monk who was also present, said he fully agreed, and cited some Sanskrit scriptures in evidence. These state that when a realized person dies, *prana,* the vital energy, dissolves into the Infinite, while for everyone else the bubble of their dream lives on.

At this point, my master exclaimed, "You are absolutely right! What you say is correct. It is the happiest, the most joyous moment, because," he said, tapping his chest lightly with both hands, "this body is a prison!"

The death of Swami Chidananda was an intense moment in my life; I was turned at all times toward the Infinite and the world seemed to hold no interest for me. Eleven days after Swamiji's death, I dreamed I was in his house in Dehradun. The monks who looked after him during his last years took me by the arm and led me into the room where he lived at the end of his life. Suddenly, my master appeared before me. I was the only one to see him. He was of the same nature as "I." It was still him, the man I had known on earth, yet he was also the Father. In silence, Swamiji made a wave with his hand, his palm facing toward me. I immediately understood: it was a teaching from the Infinite that said, as it had done to Mary and Mary Magdalene when they went to Jesus's tomb to anoint his body, "Why seek ye the living among the dead?"

WHAT YOU ARE LIES BETWEEN TWO THOUGHTS

Your thoughts and your perception of the world appear to be an uninterrupted flow, but, in fact, the process resembles what happens at the movies. When you are watching a movie it appears to flow continuously, but when you look at the filmstrip you can see the gaps between each image.

The world of forms and the apparent existence of time and space are perceived by your consciousness as images we call "thoughts." Between two thoughts, there is a kind of anchor point that you need to find in order to "be."

This point is revealed, it cannot be discovered from the standpoint of identification with names and forms, nor can it be discovered through techniques or practices of any kind.

I was talking to Swami Brahmananda one day and used the term "the others." He looked at me keenly and said, "What others?" I was stunned. For years, I had been reading in the scriptures and hearing sages proclaim that God alone is, but I had to acknowledge that even though I believed it intellectually, I was still not truly convinced since I still thought there was "me" and "the others."

I spent the rest of the day in deep thought and meditation, trying to see how I could feel that there were no other people. I went to sleep that night without having found the answer. But when I woke up the next morning, the point of being that separates deep sleep from the waking state revealed itself. My direct experience was "All Is God." I was aware of having been given a priceless gift, aware also of the importance of understanding it so that I could recognize it in the waking state. The revelation gave me all the time I needed, and this is how I discovered how to "be" in the present moment, where it is self-evident that "God Alone Is" and that there are no "others."

An authentic spiritual guide, a strong desire for the truth and patience are the necessary ingredients on the path to awakening.

ZERO EGO

Zero ego does not mean that you are going to disappear! Your true body is interiority, whose nature is Consciousness. When you have sufficiently ripened in that reality, you realize that what you had mistaken for individual consciousness is, in fact, the divine Consciousness you have always been. Your idea of being a person is an artificial creation, produced by the impressions made on you by the external world, in which you believe you will find happiness. This belief creates a wave on the calm ocean of your consciousness, a wave that then multiplies exponentially as a result of the actions born of your desires. This disturbance prevents you from being able to see and benefit from the plenitude of the immortal Self that you are.

Imagine a man in the desert who is dying of thirst and has an inexhaustible supply of water in a bottle attached to his belt. When he sees an oasis, a mirage, he tries to jump into the mirage to quench his thirst. Every time he jumps, a drop of water spurts from the bottle and moistens his lips, which makes him believe that the water comes from the mirage. In the same way, people believe that they can quench their thirst for fulfillment by seeking happiness in the outside world. This mirage reflects on the Consciousness that you are and creates a further mirage, maya, the veil of ignorance, which makes you believe you are an individual. This is how the ego is born.

The problem lies not in the senses themselves but in your belief that through them you can find happiness. It is normal for a married man to have relations with his wife. But if he is constantly looking at other women and believes that his happiness lies in having affairs, he obtains a fleeting moment of satisfaction that he then pays for with an addiction to the habit. Repeated unfaithfulness creates a new "him," a liar, who is easily irritated, perhaps violent, or capable even of murder to defend his mirage-identity. To rid himself of the habit, he will have to devote himself to life's true purpose: to discover where he is one with God.

There are people who say, "That's all very well, but I am of this world and I live in this world!" Which is equivalent to saying, "I am this body of flesh and blood." Such people are trapped in a mirage-identity that has nothing to do with reality. You are not this mass of skin, muscle, blood, and bone, nor are you your five senses, nor your intelligence—these will all perish. As for the world, you cannot take it with you to the grave! Nevertheless, at the death of the body, this mirage-identity continues to vibrate with the idea "My happiness lies in the senses!" and this prevents you, once again, from obtaining the plenitude that you are. "I want to live!" you cry, but you will have to wait a long time before obtaining the precious gift of a human life, which is the only way you can be released from this bondage.

Wake up! You are the divine Spirit. When you awaken, fear, death, misery, loneliness, and boredom no longer hold sway over you. To be anchored in the Infinite is the highest expression of God's love, the highest prayer, the greatest service, and the greatest force manifested on earth. Being anchored in the Infinite is to bear witness to the truth.

The more you practice feeling the presence of God, the more you realize that it is the source of joy. It is this that quenches your thirst; not the joys of the world, which are mere fleeting reflections.

Q: So should we remain unmoved even by beauty and joy?

A: Seekers of the truth practice seeing that the whole world is a manifestation of God, that every name and form has its place within "I Am," and this makes them happy at all times. For the ignorant, beauty is inseparable from likes and dislikes, and happiness depends on what they can obtain within the context of their preferences. What is beauty, how do you measure it, what criteria do you use? Look at the question in the light of "I Am" and learn to contemplate unity in diversity.

Q: If the world no longer exerts any hold over me and if nothing affects me, what motivation do I have to help those in need?

A: What a strange question! Do you need motivation to help others? What is happening to you is that your consciousness is growing aware of the price of awakening to divine Consciousness. You are frightened of letting go and this puts you on the defensive—which is completely normal! Don't be frightened. Practice what is being shared with you here. You will discover that nothing is insurmountable and that your motivation to serve is not in any way affected.

HOW TO REALIZE GOD

One day, tired of not being able to find "I," I went to Swami Brahmananda.

"Swamiji," I said, "I give up looking for 'I.' I believe I am one with God. I don't know where or how, but I believe it." Swamiji gave me a penetrating look and said, "That's it! There is nothing else!"

Realization begins with what you believe yourself to be. It takes time for your concept of being a person, and your belief in the reality of the world of name and form, to dissolve. To this end, settle yourself in the cable car of His peace and see that everything and everyone is part of this peace; always question your actions and bear witness on earth to the divine love that you are. Say, "Father, all I want, to the exclusion of everything else, is to be revealed where I am one with You." Then anchor yourself in the conviction: "I and my Father are one and one only," and be patient. That's it, there is nothing else!

Q: I don't understand "I don't know where." Can it be anywhere other than inside you?

A: "I Am" in you is what water is to the wave: it is its essence, its interiority. "I Am" is your sense of soul, which is an inward experience. The Spirit itself cannot be felt. The Spirit, the "I," is where you are one with the Infinite, in the same way that a wave, when it lives in communion with its "waterness," discovers where it is one with the vast ocean. Your sense of "I Am" is created by your idea of being a physical person. "I" is the divine being that you are, which cannot be the object of an experience or a feeling.

Q: So where is it then?

A: Where there is awareness. Is awareness inside or outside you?

Q: Neither.

A: Exactly! When, through communion with "I Am," you find "I," then you discover where you are one with Bhagavan, one with the Infinite; and you realize that what you had thought was your individual consciousness was, in fact, the divine Consciousness you have always been.

Q: If I've understood correctly, as long as I perceive something, then I'm in "I Am." When I'm in "I," there is no longer any sense of perception, there is only being.

A: Yes! "I," the Spirit, cannot be an object of perception: it is the divine Being that you are. There is a point of being in the here and now that you must find. But in fact, you cannot "find" it: it is revealed to those who sincerely seek it.

REALIZATION AND PERFECTION

Q: When someone has realized the Self, do they still have to control their emotions and desires, like ordinary people?

A: No, it is different. Realized beings have discovered the infinite source of joy and for them the choice is clear. After a long search, they have discovered the true fount of plenitude and can draw on it directly. There is, however, a residual karma or *prarabdha,* which is the remaining traces of identification with the physical body and the dreams that go with it. Prarabdha karma can be compared to the movement of a ball that, when thrown into the air, bounces back with decreasing momentum until it comes to a complete stop. For "ordinary" people, the movement is kept going by their belief that happiness can be found in the external world. This belief, which imprisons them, is traditionally compared to an endlessly turning wheel, the wheel of samsara. In realized beings, who are anchored in the Infinite and whose residual attachments have been consumed by the fire of the Spirit, the wheel goes on turning simply through inertia, but the movement itself is not sustained.

Q: When a realized being makes a mistake, is the ego responsible?

A: What is the ego? It is the "I-thought," the product of an egoic territory whose nature is to act egotistically. A realized being is like a storm blowing itself out; there may be a few remaining gusts of egoic territory, but once he or she has been exposed to the Spirit for long enough, there is no going back to the "ego."

Nevertheless, because this world in all its multiplicity is imperfect, mistakes are inevitable. This is illustrated in the Mahabharata, when at the end of the last battle, Krishna, the Almighty incarnate, who had sworn not to intervene on either side of the battle lines, goes back on his word. When he sees an arrow aimed at his friend and disciple, Arjuna, he drags his foot in order to lower his chariot, and the arrow, instead of piercing Arjuna's head, glances off his helmet. This was, of course, part of the divine plan, but the episode reminds us that nothing on earth can be perfect.

The divine Father, however, is perfect. When you are anchored in the Infinite, a profound transformation, difficult to put into words, occurs. My master, Swami Chidananda, described it as an ascension in "being" at every moment and in all our actions, which alone makes Self-knowledge possible. Another expression sometimes used is "growing in saintliness." Ramana Maharshi realized God at sixteen. At that age, traces of what he had been previously may still have been potentially active. Sixty years later, there was nothing left of these traces; there was no difference between his actions and those of the Spirit. Being anchored in the Infinite had made him its pure reflection.

PROTECTION

Death is a force of God, called Yama in India. Every mortal being is subject to this force, and nothing in the world of name and form can escape it. But you are Spirit, which is immortal. "Weapons cut It not, fire burns It not, water wets

It not, wind dries It not."⁴ Your true being is eternal and unchanging. It is the body and mind with which you identify that are mortal, and subject therefore to death—at least in appearance. But if you love God and abide in His presence, you are born to the immortal body of "I Am" and Yama cannot touch you on the basis of karma alone. After you have wasted so many years looking for happiness in the outside world, do you really think God would allow the body you have at last used to answer His call to be subject to the laws of the mortal world? Often cited is the example of the man whose karma was to have his head cut off and whose hat was snatched away instead.

One day in Haiti, I went with my father to collect a check for the sale of some water purifiers. We were sitting in the waiting room when two *tonton macoutes* came in. These men were under the pay of the dictator and were ready to murder at the drop of a hat—a sideways look in their direction was enough to get you killed. One of the men was wearing civilian clothes and the other was in uniform. The man wearing uniform went into the director's office, leaving his machine gun on the bench next to his colleague. I had not realized that the man in civilian clothes was also a tonton macoute, and said to him, "That's odd, leaving his gun behind like that!"

The man turned to me and said in Creole, "Do you want me to try it on you?"

Without thinking, I spread my arms and, pointing to my chest, said, "If you think you can kill me by killing this body, go ahead, shoot me here!"

Then something strange happened: the man began to tremble all over. "Who are you?" he said. "You're an *ogun* [a voodoo sorcerer], is that what you are? What are you doing to me?"

What had happened was simply that the man had felt "I Am." Those who turn to God experience "I Am" as peace and silence, but an ignorant person experiences it as fear, a fear that is even greater if the person is cruel and merciless. The man had mistaken me for a sorcerer and thought I was the cause of what he was experiencing. In fact it was the divine Mother saying, "If you dare lay a hand on him, watch out!"

This experience showed me that what the scriptures say, and what I am sharing with you now, is true: God *is*. That is why faith is central to all spiritual practice. Faith is the light of the divine Consciousness that you are. No experience is foreign to you or, to be precise, to the life in you that absorbs all. When nothing can disturb your inner stillness, "He that sees" awakens, and at that point you are released from the bondage of fear.

LIFE IS AN ILLNESS

We often refuse to accept illness or the effect it has on us. Why fight against a situation you cannot change? This does not mean that you become passive—you obviously have to do everything possible to regain your health—but when His will manifests in the form of illness, it is an opportunity for you to be that on which the illness is occurring.

The entire visible universe is nothing but a sneeze of God, an illness that has fastened itself onto the ocean of Consciousness that you are in order to restore you to yourself. You, the divine Spirit, have caught a cold! I can already hear your objections: "But, Swamiji, you don't realize the importance of the universe!" To which I reply, "And you don't realize the importance of the ocean of divine Consciousness that you are!"

THE POWER OF THE SPIRIT

The Spirit that you are has a twofold power: it loves and believes. The cinema of your life is determined by how the Spirit chooses to invest itself; in other words, what you believe and how you love. Take, for example, the famous American General George S. Patton, nicknamed "Old Blood and Guts." What Patton liked best was to lead his men into battle; he lived for fighting and defeating his enemies. Apparently, he also believed in reincarnation and was convinced that he had fought as a Roman legionary in the great battles of antiquity. He longed to return to those times.

In his next dream, a man such as Patton could be a soldier in the armies of Alexander, Julius Caesar, or Genghis Khan. The Spirit continues in the direction of whatever had dominated a previous life. As long as the Spirit is invested in the unreal, you can drift indefinitely from one dream to another, and this is how the cinema of life is perpetuated. Even though, paradoxically, there is only one life and one "I Am."

Q: How do you go about changing the way you invest the Spirit? In the end, doesn't God decide everything? For example, I realize that I had no choice but to come on this retreat. It happened almost in spite of myself.

A: What God are you talking about? A God who decides everything, while you remain trapped in the dream with no way of escaping? In that case, where is your dignity of being? The God you are talking about is a mind-made God of your imagination. If God did everything, you would have no freedom whatsoever and there would be a separation between you and That which is free; because God is, in essence, absolutely free. Can you imagine a wave separate from the ocean? No! You are Spirit and the Spirit is free; there is no separation between you and Him. At the level of Spirit, you have total free will, and it is this that confers dignity on your being.

If you awaken to the truth in this lifetime and still want to come back and live in the dream, your wish will be granted. It is you, the Spirit, that decides. Of course, as long as you remain in the dream, the dream appears to be real, and at the level of dream identity, at the level of the person you think you are, you have no free will. But as soon as you realize that space, time, and all the images and people in the dream are contained in "I Am," how can anything still impress you? And when everything, including you, is absorbed by God, what is left? All that is left is "I," the Spirit, the Infinite. Then comes the revelation, confirmed by sages of every tradition, that this world, this dream, this cinema, never existed. Only He Is.

Q: I don't understand how Patton could be reincarnated and come back as a Roman. Everything to do with life at the time of the Romans has disappeared; there are only a few ruins left!

A: You believe that time as perceived by human beings is an absolute truth, yet the laws of physics show that time is relative. If you spend one year in a space capsule traveling close to the speed of light, several years will have gone by on earth—your younger brother will have caught up with you in age! The same goes for space; the light from a star that travels near a black hole describes a curve because space is curved. Welcome to the world of Einsteinian relativity!

The laws that govern the natural world distort your perception of reality and truth. Is God conditioned by time and space, or is space-time contained in Him? What we think happened ten billion years ago is not in the past for God but in the eternal present of his being. And the same goes for the future.

This life, which you believe to be so real, is a dream, just like the dreams you have at night. Imagine you are an archaeologist with a passionate interest in Ancient Greece. It is quite possible that you might dream one night about your great interest, and in your dream you find yourself on the agora, where you bump into Pericles, Socrates, or Herodotus. Perhaps the Parthenon is being built and you meet Callicrates and Phidias, who share their latest plans with you. All this seems very real until you wake up to the now. A dream such as this is perfectly possible, so it is also perfectly possible that when the archaeologist dies he might find himself living at the time of Pericles, because his next dream will unfold in accordance with what had filled his inner world in a previous life. It is not really a question of going back in time.

At present you are dreaming, and your dream is the result of how you have invested the light that you are. It is this light that gives the dream images an appearance of truth, and in "I Am" the supply of images is limitless.

EVERYTHING IS PERFECT

The world is a mirror that reflects what you are. To discover what in you is perfect, you must see the world as an expression of His perfection. Any imperfection you see is your own. When you perceive the world as an expression of "I Am," that which in you is perfect—which is the true "I" that coincides with the Spirit—gradually emerges.

I can already hear your objection: "What about wars, genocide, torture, and all the other atrocities that go on every day? You can't say that they are perfect!" Of course not. Yet they are an expression of His perfection. Why? Say, for example, that you had been born into a Nazi family and joined the Hitler Youth—can you guarantee that you would not have become a good Nazi, with everything it implies? As a consequence, sooner or later, you would undergo the same suffering that you had inflicted. Just as when you slam your fist into a concrete wall, you suffer an equal and opposite reaction, which lands you in the hospital with broken fingers. Even though the individual soul is not what you are, as long as you remain trapped in the dream you suffer the consequences of your actions, both good and bad. What is valid at the individual level is valid at a collective level.

People who judge the world believe unconsciously that they are above what they judge, and think they could never behave in the same way. Yet the simple fact of judging demonstrates the opposite, because people who are ignorant of interiority and mistake the world for ultimate reality are shaped by their social and cultural environment, as well as by their spiritual level. Judging shows a lack of trust in life and is a way of saying that God makes mistakes. Perfection is certainly not of this world, yet the world is an expression of His perfection and how it evolves is not in your hands. Recognizing this frees you from the dream. If, on the other hand, you believe that the world is a collection of molecules that have come together by chance, that science explains everything and is the sole reality, you are totally trapped. You live in complete ignorance of the principle of life, of which this universe is but a ripple.

Q: But we still have responsibility as human beings!

A: The problem of human responsibility begins with the egoic territory, which is the root cause of all selfish behavior. If you criticize war, are you criticizing it from the standpoint of "I Am" or from an egoic territory? It is right to fight against a Hitler, but to rape, pillage, and murder women and children is not. One of the main causes of injustice is anger, and anger contains the seeds of war. If you give up being angry, instead of seeing war you will be able see what lies at its root. The only way to achieve this is to remain connected to inner peace and become, in the words of St. Francis of Assisi, an instrument of His peace.

Q: You are talking about the inner world, but as individuals we have to live in society, and meanwhile life goes on.

A: You talk as if the outer world excluded the inner world. Learn to live in harmony with life, even in the midst of your everyday activities, and you will live in harmony with the whole world. Would you renounce the Eternal in favor of this world? You have not been given human life just to worry about what is going on around you. At the time of death, the world cannot help you and no one is going to offer to take your place. Inner life is the vehicle that carries you back to your true home. Use it to awaken instead of filling it with ideas that are going to perish with the body. Live in the world but offer all your actions to God, remembering with each breath that everything is His expression. Rome was not built in a day, but everything comes with practice and perseverance.

FAITH AND BELIEF

Q: "You have to follow the instructions of a teacher," "You must believe"—I find all this a bit disturbing. In any case, for me belief has nothing to do with faith.

A: Belief has everything to do with faith, because faith is, by definition, an act of believing. You can say, "I don't believe in God," but in that case, let me ask you, with what do you believe you don't believe? "Believing" has no opposite because it is an absolute principle of life. You cannot not believe. For you, the word "faith" has been colored by experience, but it is nonetheless an act of Consciousness, an act of the light, of the Spirit that you are. What I am sharing with you now is not about believing or not believing, it is about having the direct experience of that which in you believes, which is also that which in you loves, that which in you knows, and that which in you is. This is "awakening to the divine Self."

You cannot awaken to the divine Self by following your own recipe. When you bake a cake, you have to follow the instructions carefully or the result may not be successful. I am not saying you must do this; I am giving you the recipe for awakening to the Spirit, which was given to me by my divine master, and I can assure you that it works! Then it is up to you to take it or leave it.

Q: I sometimes feel what I call a "presence." It can happen anywhere—in the kitchen or when I'm out for a walk.

A: Presence is the path but not the goal. The test of the spiritual path is love, and how it reflects in your actions toward others. You awaken to divine love by following the recipe of the sages, who all basically prescribe the same method.

184

DIVINE WILL

Q: If I've understood correctly, our mistakes are due to the egoic territory and to the fact that we shine the light that we are onto something other than "I Am." But it's also said that everything is the fruit of divine will, so aren't mistakes also somehow an expression of God's game?

A: You can say that everything is an expression of divine will if you look on the entire universe as moving inexorably toward its ultimate source, the Infinite. From this perspective everything, apart from humanity, is advancing step by step toward its goal, aligned with "I Am" and benefiting from the plenitude of the Absolute. Seen from this angle, everything happens according to His will. Humanity, however, is not aligned with "I Am," and is therefore the source of a great deal of disharmony. But even this disharmony is part of the inexorable march toward the Infinite, in spite of the fact that some people are regressing on the path for a while because of misdeeds.

But there is another way of looking at things, and here are two stories that illustrate it.

Once upon a time, there was a village woman who longed for children. She had been married for several years and was beginning to fear she might be barren. She heard of a devout man to whom God appeared every evening, so, gathering up her courage, she went to the man and asked if she could serve him.

After a few days, the man turned to her and said, "Why have you come? What do you want from me?"

"Maharaj," replied the woman, "I've heard that you see God every evening, please would you ask Him if I will ever have children?"

The man agreed, "I'll have a word with Him this very night."

That evening when God appeared, the man said to him, "Lord, you who are omniscient, could you tell me if this poor woman will one day have the child she yearns for?"

"No," replied God, "it is not in her karma to bear children in this lifetime."

The man broke the news to the woman the next morning. "My poor child, God is categorical; there is no question of you having a child in this lifetime." Dismayed, the woman decided to put an end to her life and set off to the river that ran along the valley. On the way, she heard a voice gently calling her name and stopped to see who it was. A sadhu appeared before her.

"Where are you going, my child?" he asked.

What's the point of answering, thought the woman, *since God has already decided my fate.*

But the sage persisted, and the woman eventually told him what she was planning to do and why. "Oh, Mother!" he exclaimed. "Who told you that you could not have a child? You will have not one, but three! Now go home and get ready for the little ones."

While the sage was speaking, the woman felt enveloped by a sense of deep peace that emanated from his presence. Restored to calm, she went home comforted.

Nine months later, she gave birth to a boy. The following year a little girl saw the light of day, and the third year, another boy. When the children were old enough to walk, the woman decided to take them to meet the sage. She searched for him in vain, and decided to seek out the devout man instead.

When the man saw her with three small children, he could not believe his eyes. "Hey!" he cried. "Whose children are these?"

"Yours, Maharaj," said the woman, "because it is indirectly thanks to you that I received these blessings."

"What!" said the man incredulously. "Against God's word? But that is not possible! He'll be hearing from me tonight!"

And indeed, when God made his usual appearance, the devout man did not try to hide his annoyance. "Do you realize, Lord, three children! You told me she couldn't have any. You were definite about it! What have you made me look like? People are going to think I'm a charlatan and say that I don't really see you. My reputation is ruined!"

God listened patiently to these recriminations and said, "I owe you an explanation. I didn't lie to you—it was not in the woman's karma to have children, but her path happened to cross the path of a sage established in the Infinite. When such a man makes a pronouncement, it comes true. You see, you run after me, but I run after him!"

The second story illustrates the same truth but from a different angle.

There was once a man who, after repeating the name of God for many years, was at last granted a vision of the Lord, and this made him feel very proud. He worshipped God in the form of Lord Krishna, who had become his constant companion, and when Lord Krishna saw his devotee's head swollen with pride, he decided to teach him a lesson. When he next appeared to the man, he told him about an annual gathering of sages that was taking place in a neighboring village.

"Next week," he said, "wise men from throughout the kingdom are going to be tested. Perhaps it would be a good idea for you to participate, to see where you stand in relation to them. What do you think?"

The man eagerly agreed. He was sure that because of his vision of the Lord he would be recognized as a sage of the highest order. When the day arrived, he took his place at the gathering.

In charge of the test was a potter, who tested his pots by tapping the unglazed vessels with a stick. If they rang true, he knew the pots were properly fired. If they made a dull sound, he sent them back to be recycled. Strange as it may seem, the same test was used on the head of the sages.

Armed with a stick, the potter began. The first head rang out with a pure sound. "Oh, very good, Maharaj," said the potter, "truly excellent!" and continued down the line. The second, third, fourth, and fifth heads all rang true, but when it came to the turn of our Krishna devotee, the potter tapped his head and a dull note resounded.

"I'm afraid, Maharaj," said the potter, somewhat embarrassed, "that a little more maturity is required; a little something is still missing."

"How dare you!" exclaimed our man, white with rage. "Don't you know that I see God? Don't you forget that!" and with those words he strode out of the gathering.

When Krishna next made an appearance, the man told him, in no uncertain terms, how displeased he was.

"After all, Lord, I see you, don't I? It's not nothing to have a vision. How can they say I'm not mature enough?"

"I understand," said Krishna, "but there may be some truth in what they said. To clear up any doubt, I think you should go and see the sadhu who lives in a hut not far from the temple in the next village over. He will be able to clarify matters."

So our man set off to the temple. When he arrived, he started back in shock at the sight of the sadhu lying on the floor, his feet resting on the *shiva lingam,* symbol of the Infinite.

"Hey, you!" he cried. "Do you realize what you're doing? Can't you see where you've put your feet?"

"Oh, my goodness!" said the sadhu. "You're right," and he turned to face the opposite direction. At that moment, the shiva lingam disappeared and reappeared under his feet. This happened several times: whenever the sadhu changed places, the lingam reappeared under his feet.

"I don't understand, "said the man, "what is going on?"

"My friend," said the sadhu, "do you not know that God is everywhere?" and he returned to his contemplation.

When our man next saw Krishna, his ego was considerably deflated. "Krishna," he said, "please explain, I don't understand."

"You see," said Krishna, "your problem is that you think I am here and that you are there."

These stories illustrate that the ocean of infinite love we call God is different from the idea we have of Him. God makes Himself available to us in the form of "I Am," the current that flows to the Infinite and can be called "God's will"; but neither the experience of "I Am" nor the vision of God are the ultimate goal. Even if the Immaculate Conception appeared before us at this very moment, however beautiful and inspiring the vision might be, there is still more. The supreme goal is, in the words of Jesus, to be revealed where "I and my Father are one and one alone." All the Almighty wants is to take you there.

It is you, the divine Spirit, who chooses what to love and believe; you who sustains the cinema of life and decides to believe you are a person. So, yes, everything is an expression of the divine will.

DON'T CHASE AFTER WHAT YOU ALREADY ARE

Q: Sometimes I feel I've had enough of playing all these different roles, enough of worry and anxiety. I'd like to be in a state of joy, of bliss, all the time.

A: But in the here and now you are in that state of joy. It is what you are. You don't have to wait to be in it!

Q: It's as though there were these veils. . . .

A: What veils? You know that you are sitting here right now, don't you? You know that you are listening to me? You know there are people sitting behind you? That it is sunny outside? Do you have to do anything to know this? That which knows is in the here and now, isn't it? With what do you know all this?

Q: God knows it.

A: Can you see That which in you sees?

Q: No.

A: Indeed, That which sees cannot be seen. It is divine Consciousness, the Absolute that you are. The person you think you are is an expression of life; it is part of "I Am," the mirror that reveals to you what you are. But That which sees both the person and "I Am" is joy and plenitude. At the moment you are like someone walking into the sun whose shadow is running behind trying to catch up. You never can catch up, so stop running! Know that you are That. Be still and be happy. The world is a great game, the garden of the Child God—at least for those who have not forgotten what they truly are.

WHAT MAKES US BEGIN TO SEE?

Q: "It is She who does everything." OK, but the more I look at things from that perspective, the more I see all my mistakes!

A: That is interesting. What makes us begin to "see"? When you give up the idea of being a person and adopt the view "It is not I who am doing, but Thee," you move into another dimension; you place yourself on the level of "I Am" and live in harmony with the divine. What "sees" in you is, in reality, *He*. As long as you are trapped in the idea "I am doing," you cannot see your mistakes, which is why Jesus said, "Father, forgive them, for they know not what they do."[5]

Whenever the urge "I want" arises, a Big Bang occurs and the cosmic force of avidya maya, ignorance, draws you outward and compels you to seek happiness in the external world. But gradually you develop the capacity to see the movement "I want" as it arises. This is a step toward awakening, because the intellect is not capable of seeing this movement at its source, nor can it see any mistakes.

That which sees cannot be controlled, nor can it be grasped as an experience. That which in you sees is none other than the Almighty, which no word can describe, and yet it is your true Self.

ATTACHMENT AND DETACHMENT

Q: If all human beings were awakened, would it be the end of the human race?

A: Your question presupposes that you understand what it means to be awakened. Begin by awaking to the Spirit that you are! Where are you when you are in the state of deep sleep? Where are your friends, children, or parents? Does their absence bother you? In deep sleep there is no one and nothing and yet you happily spend several hours a night in that state. What for you is the state of deep sleep when you are asleep, is for me the waking state; and, seen from this state, God Alone Is. The idea of "other people" exists only as long as you remain identified with the world of name and form. Awaken and the question no longer arises.

Q: But that won't stop me continuing to live in the world; I'll still be able to see, hear, talk, move?

A: Absolutely!

Q: So this world does have some reality?

A: "I Am" is real; existence in you is real. But if you say "I'm a woman, I'm forty-five years old, I'm a teacher, a mother, I'm French," who are you really? Which of those definitions is the right one? In reality, none of them. In deep sleep you are none of those things. Before you were born you were none of them and after your death none will remain. And they are not what you are at this moment.

Your attachment to names and forms and what you imagine to be happiness make you want to go on believing in this world. So belief is there, faith is there, but they are not pointed in the right direction. You need to change course, detach yourself from the world of definitions, of "my job," "my daughter," and attach yourself to God, to reality.

The problem does not lie in the world itself, but in the fact that the divine, boundless love that you are is confined by your narrow beliefs. Expansion of your Consciousness will manifest when you abide in the principle of life that absorbs all into Himself.

WAVES NEED DO NOTHING TO BE WATER

Q: When you talk of "denying" the world, is it the result of a process by which you take the reality of the world apart, as it were?

A: The Isha Upanishad opens with the invocation:

Om purmamadah purnamidam purnat
purnamudachyate purnasya purnamadaya
purnameva vashishyate . . .
This world is plenitude, God is plenitude,
If you deny the world, His plenitude alone remains . . .

These words from the Vedas can be interpreted on different levels. On the human level, it means that when you renounce the idea of finding fulfillment in the external world you obtain contentment. On the level of "I Am," plenitude arises in your life like the morning sun when you deny the truth of the world of name and form, while recognizing that this truth belongs to "I Am," to the body of the inner Christ—as do you. In the final stage, when you are awakened, the Spirit that you are understands that "God Alone Is." At this point, everything is seen as the play of Consciousness. Everything that happens is a reflection, a dream, a play of forms that has never been separate from Consciousness. In order to understand this, wake up!—because you will never be able to understand it on the human level.

Q: Is it a kind of wonderment?

A: It is far more than wonder, which is a human emotion. No words can describe the direct experience of the Self. In the same way that in deep sleep your mind and speech are absorbed and cannot express the experience, so when you recognize the state of deep sleep in the waking state, and "I" is revealed, it is impossible to describe. The only word you can use is "Spirit." In this instance, the word is not used to describe the nature of the Infinite; it designates the meeting point between humans and the Infinite. At this point, the mysteries of life are revealed to awakened beings, who realize that the Spirit was always there, at every moment of their lives. Waves need do nothing to be water. Nevertheless . . .

FREE WILL

If you look at the way your life has unfolded, you realize that there is nothing to change: the script was already written. And yet you believe you have free will, because in the Absolute you are the divine, free, eternal, glorious Consciousness. The problem is that you direct your light onto identification with body and mind. You are neither body nor mind. The person you think you are is a fiction; it belongs to the cinema of your life, which unfolds according to how you believe, love, and act. You let yourself be carried away by the universal, impersonal force "I want," which pulls you into the external world and makes you lose sight of your true nature. It is "I want" that creates the egoic territory and enslaves you. And it is the egoic territory that makes you believe that the world is real and that it will bring you happiness.

By directing your light today in the world of name and form, you are generating tomorrow's movie, so how can there be free will ? Although the cinema of life is not real, it is nevertheless governed by the law of causality, of karma—action and reaction, cause and effect—which traps you as soon as you believe in the truth of the names and forms on the movie screen. Because you become what you believe and love, this limits you to the world of name and form. And you, who are the light of the Eternal, you who are Spirit, forget the freedom and bliss of your true nature.

Before the crucifixion, Jesus already knew what was going to happen to him. Although he cannot be compared to an ordinary man, Jesus's life was already written. The absence of free will that this implies should not disturb —you because, on the level of the divine Spirit that you are, you are free. On the physical level of body and mind, which is not what you are, you are not free; but the body and mind are nevertheless there to carry you through this world, like travelers journeying briefly through time and space. When Pontius Pilate asked Jesus if he was king of the Jews, Jesus replied, "My kingdom is not of this world." What was true for him is true for you. He is the divine Spirit, as are you.

The world is nothing but an illusion, a mere reflection in divine Consciousness. Its substance is real, but the appearances and forms it takes are not, just like in a dream. You have all probably had a dream that seemed so real that when you woke up the dream stayed with you. Yet every one of the people and events in your dream, as well as the person you thought you were, were all within your consciousness. You had no control over what happened and no way of changing the script.

On this subject, Swami Brahmananda described the following experience:

One day, I was at Haridwar, in an ashram near the Ramakrishna Mission Hospital at Kankhal. An aged Swamiji was conducting a bhajan *[devotional song]. I was told that the Swamiji was a revered mahatma who was not only a* vedavit *[a knower of the Vedas], but also a* brahma-nishtha *[one who is established in Brahman]. I attended the inspiring kirtans of the great Swamiji, which concluded with the song of Sri Sadasiva Brahmendra Swami—sarvam brahmamayam [All Is God]. There was perfect silence, a divine peace and calm for some time. Then many asked questions, and Swamiji answered them to their entire satisfaction. Some raised their doubts on very intricate problems of Vedanta, and Swamiji Maharaj cleared them with ease and clarity. In the end the following conversation took place between Swamiji and myself:*

Brahmananda: Most revered Maharaj, certain scriptures and sages like your Holiness say that this waking state is only a long dream. But, Maharaj, I am unable to understand how it can be as unreal and fleeting as a dream. Now, I am sitting before your Holiness and you are speaking to me. How can this be a dream?

Swamiji: Yes, I can understand your difficulty. You must have shraddha, an unshakable faith in God, scriptures, and sages and their sayings, and also in the goal promised by them, which is nothing less than complete freedom and eternal Peace, the Peace that transcends intellectual understanding. The English word "faith" means trust, belief, confidence. The Sanskrit word shraddha, which I have used now in this context, means all these and much more, and it relates to the Self. . . . So I want you to have faith, shraddha, in the scriptures and Masters also. I tell you from my own experience that this state now we are experiencing, appearing as a waking state to both of us, is not a waking state; it is a dream.

Brahmananda: Maharaj, then am I sleeping now? One dreams only when one is asleep.

Swamiji: Yes. You are sleeping and also dreaming. This satsang, including you and me, is in your dream. I tell you again, I am stating the truth based on my experience, which has the concurrence of the scriptures. Believe me. Have shraddha. Reflect over what I have said. You will realize the truth that all the three states—waking, dream, and deep sleep—are dream only, and the Self is the substratum for them, even as the water is the substratum for the disturbed ocean with boisterous billows, mild ripples, foam, and bubbles, and also for the calm ocean.

My doubt was not cleared. But the Swamiji suddenly left the satsang hall and people started dispersing. I also moved out of the hall and was walking on the road, reflecting as to how the waking state could be a dream state.

And lo! I woke up from my dream. I found myself on my bed in my room at Rishikesh. The whole dream was very clear in my mind, to the most minute detail. The train of thoughts that passed through my mind then was something like this: Now I am in the waking state. I was dreaming till now. When I was dreaming I mistook it for the waking state. What the Swamiji in the dream said was true. He said more than once that he was telling the truth based on his own experience. I was wrong in thinking it was a waking state. It was a mistake on my part to have doubted his wise words. Now I realize my mistake. It was a dream and not a waking state. The present waking state also must be like that. It must be a dream, and I mistakenly think that it is a real waking state. My Gurudev [Swami Sivananda] also has said to me, not once or twice but a number of times, that the waking state is a long dream. But I had doubted his statement; I was not convinced. Now I realize that my Gurudev's statement is similar to the dream-Swamiji's statement. I should entertain no more doubt about it. I have learnt a lesson from my dream last night. I should not repeat the mistake again. Let me go to my Gurudev to get further clarification and confirmation. . . .

In the morning, I got up early and ran to Gurudev's kutir. His Holiness was then just coming out of his kutir after his morning meditation. I immediately fell at his feet and paid my usual obeisance. He accosted me with his usual smiling face and said:

Gurudev: *Oh, my dear disciple, how is it that you are here so early today? Have you anything special to tell me, any doubt about your last night's dream?*

Brahmananda: *Yes, Gurudev. Last night I had a dream, and the experience there has convinced me of your repeated instructions about the nature of this waking state. (Then I explained to him in detail all about the dream and the train of thoughts I'd had after waking.)*

Gurudev: I already know about your dream. Now what is your conclusion?

Brahmananda: I have now come to the firm conclusion that the waking state is a dream. I have learned the truth. I have no more doubt that both the so-called waking and dreaming states that we experience every day are only dreams, passing experiences, transient in nature, without any substantiality.

Gurudev: Who is the experiencer of the two dreams?

Brahmananda: The visva *[witness of the waking state] and* taijasa *[witness of the dream state].*

Gurudev: Who are you then? What is "your" place, the "I" in you?

Brahmananda: The "I" is the witness of the two states.

Gurudev: What about the third state, the deep sleep state?

Brahmananda: The "I" is the witness of that experience also.

Gurudev: Was there any experience in deep sleep to be witnessed by the "I"?

Brahmananda: Certainly not. Then how can the "I" be said to be the witness, when there is nothing to be witnessed?

Gurudev: Yes. That is exactly what I want you to realize. The "I" is not even the witness. Are you clear about this? The sakshi bhava *[the attitude of witness] also has to be transcended.*

Brahmananda: By your grace, things are becoming clear. I am now certain that the "I" transcends the witness-ship in deep sleep.

Gurudev: Then, is the "I" witness during the two dream states? What have you understood of the word "dream"? Does anything happen there? Take one incident in the dream and analyze. For instance, last night did you go to Haridwar and meet that great Swamiji? No, you did not. Nothing happened. If that is the case with one incident, it must be so with all the incidents in last night's dream. It must be so in the dreams that we seem to experience every day. You are already convinced that the waking state is also a dream. Therefore, you have come to the conclusion that in both the states—the so-called waking and dream state—nothing happens, and therefore there is nothing to be witnessed by the "I." Hence, the "I" cannot be said to be a witness in all the three states. You must know that the "I" is sat-chit-ananda, *the pure Existence-Consciousness-Bliss-Absolute, during all the three states, whether it is deep sleep, without the appearance of the world, including one's own individual personality, or the two dream states, where there seems to be an appearance of the world, including one's individual personality. The "I" is like the water*

of the ocean of Consciousness, whether the ocean is calm or with waves and
ripples. This is referred to as the "cosmic waters" in some scriptures, as that
which was before the so-called Creation.[6]

It is important to reflect deeply on the characteristics of the dream state and
recognize that they apply also to the waking state. This allows the divine Consciousness that you are to come to the forefront of your life, instead of remaining in the dusty drawer of your intellect. When you awaken to the divine Self,
the question of free will no longer arises. This whole world is nothing but a reflection in divine Consciousness—in Jesus's words, the "Father." You are That.

Q: Once we've realized that this life is a dream, a cinema, what makes us want
   to go on playing in it?
A: Your focus of interest does, in fact, change: a walk in the countryside becomes more appealing than a rock concert; an evening spent chanting the
   name of God and sharing the joys of the spiritual path becomes more attractive than drinking and smoking in a bar; helping others takes up more
   of your life than going to a football or boxing match.
      Your duty is to believe in the nobility of being divine Consciousness and
   to live with the conviction that it will be revealed to you when you abide
   in communion with life. Realize that everything and everyone belongs to
   God, whom you love in the form of "I Am." When you have made room in
   your life for the divine, the dream itself is seen as an expression of God, and
   therefore as a source of joy. In this way, every image in your dream reveals
   the truth. When a baby pats a musical toy a hundred times, why does it cry
   out with joy each time? Because the toy reveals the bliss of its being and the
   baby expresses this with a cry of joy.
      It is not a question of rejecting anything; it is a question of changing the
   way you see things. Life with your husband, wife, or children should not be
   seen as a duty but as a blessing that helps you advance quickly toward liberation. "I Am" is service. Joy and contentment come from serving God by
   serving your family, friends, and neighbors—anyone you have the opportunity to serve. Serving your mother and father, insofar as they have fulfilled their role as parents, is to serve God, and is therefore a joy—even if it
   is not always easy. In this way you grow in saintliness. Your role is to bear

witness, through your actions, to the divine love that you are. And with that, be happy!

Q: I'm totally confused. The idea that the world isn't real, that there is no free will, is very disturbing.

A: It requires a certain maturity to understand these concepts. Until you have reached a certain maturity, some answers are impossible to understand. With time, however, what had once seemed incomprehensible becomes clear. But until you are firmly established in faith in God, and in the belief that this faith, this peace, is the divine, you will go on experiencing uncertainty and turmoil. Trust that when the time comes He will help you understand what is to be understood.

Meanwhile, your confusion is normal, and comes from your identification with the intellect. At some point you have to let go of the intellect if you want to arrive at more profound truths. The intellect is like a ship moored to the shore; tied to its concepts, it feels safe and happy and thinks it understands what is going on. Now I am asking you to lift anchor and set out to sea, where there are no longer any reference points. Your intellect revolts, which is understandable. Don't be afraid: when you are lost in "I Am," with total faith in God, you are in the field of the Almighty and you are completely safe. When you let go of identification with the mind, which is what chains you to the shore, you feel more alive and you radiate joy. The people around you will also be happy, because the joy you radiate is that of the divine. You then understand that it is the light of the Spirit that enables the intellect to carry out its work, and you realize that the light of the Self transcends all and that it is the substratum of the cosmos. And then all is well.

YOU ARE LOVE

I was sitting in the garden just now with one of the participants on this retreat; we were looking at the forest in the distance, at some funny little insects that reminded us of angels, and at the dandelion flowers at our feet. I asked the person if she liked the flowers. "Oh, yes!" she said. "I love dandelion flowers." This would normally be interpreted as a person's love of a flower, that is to say, a love that loves an object, with all the play of attraction and repulsion that this involves. In reality, that which in you loves the flower is not the person, it is love itself. The nature of the Spirit is love. Love is the substratum of Consciousness, and where there is love is *advaita:* "one and one only." You are That, so look at what you love and learn to be that which loves. Love is joy. Enjoy the love of God to the fullest. Sit in a garden or park and savor the drop of joy that emanates naturally from your being, and is totally independent of any object in the world.

Such moments are rare. They are an opportunity to practice being, and to drink at the fountain of joy here and now. You need joy in your life. This is not a meditation; keep your eyes wide open and let nature teach you. You see a flower? "I am that which loves." A beautiful tree? "Love." You hear birdsong? "Love." Train yourself in this manner so that when you are with people who do not attract you, you can look at them from this point of view. Understand that even in these situations, love loves and you are That.

When Pilate asked Jesus why he had come into the world, Jesus replied, "That I should bear witness unto the truth." The beauty of this answer is that it applies to everyone. You have, we all have, the opportunity to bear witness to the truth.

NOTES

INTRODUCTION: SWAMI CHIDANANDA—HIS PART IN MY LIFE

1. Luke 18:29–30 (Authorized King James Version).
2. John 14:6 (AV) .
3. "Gurudev": the name given to Swami Sivananda by his disciples.

1. A FEW BASIC PRINCIPLES

1. These themes are to be found in the *Kena, Katha, Isha, Mundaka,* and *Manduka Upanishads,* among other texts.
2. From *jeru,* "fear," and *shalom,* "peace."
3. Zech. 8:3 (AV).
4. John 10:34 (AV).
5. Exod. 3:1–20 (AV).
6. Exod. 32:6 (AV).
7. Gal. 2:20 (AV).
8. Bhagavad Gita, 2:69, translated by Swami Sivananda. Swami Sivananda, *The Bhagavad Gita,* 13th ed. (Rishikesh, India: Divine Life Society, 2003).
9. Matt. 22:21, Mark 12:17 (AV).
10. "So Jesus said to them, 'Because of your unbelief; for assuredly, I say to you, if you have faith as a mustard seed, you will say to this mountain, 'Move from here to there,' and it will move; and nothing will be impossible for you." Matt. 17:20 (AV).
11. Prov. 3:5 (AV).
12. Lev. 19:18, Matt. 19:19, Mark 12:31, Luke 10:27 (AV).
13. *Brihadaranyaka Upanishad,* Chapter V, 11th "Brahmana."

2. SPIRITUAL PRACTICE

1. John 3:3 (AV).

2. *Neti-neti*: "neither this nor that." A process of negative discrimination, found in the *Brihadaranyaka Upanishad,* which consists of rejecting the phenomenal world in order to discover what lies beyond, and to become aware that ultimate reality is "neither this, nor that."
3. Matt. 6:33 (AV).
4. Deut. 6:5, Matt. 22:37, Mark 12:30 (AV).

3. DIFFICULTIES ON THE PATH

1. Matt. 5:14 (AV).
2. Matt. 5:24 (AV).
3. Matt. 8:26 (AV).
4. Matt. 26:61 (AV).
5. Zech. 8:3 (AV).
6. Isa. 51:17 (AV).
7. Used here in its etymological sense, "to make holy," from the Latin *sacer* ("sacred," "holy") and *facere* ("to make"). To abandon or sacrifice yourself to God confers sacredness on whoever makes the "sacrifice."
8. Sanskrit word meaning "game." Creation is considered to be the game of God.
9. John 8:58 (AV).
10. John 18:36 (AV).
11. Bhagavad Gita, 2:26, translated by Swami Sivananda.
12. Matt. 5:48 (AV).
13. Matt. 12:50 (AV).

5. DAILY LIFE: RELATIONSHIPS, FAMILY, WORK

1. Luke 22:42 (AV).
2. Matt. 8:20, Luke 9:58 (AV).
3. Prov. 3:5, 3:6 (AV).
4. John 7:38 (AV).
5. John 18:37 (AV).
6. Matt. 5:39, Luke 6:29 (AV).
7. Matt. 5:38 (AV).
8. Matt. 23:27 (AV).
9. Matt. 21:12, Mark 11:15 (AV).

6. THE RELATIONSHIP WITH A TEACHER

1. Constant repetition of the name of God.
2. Meaning "Papa." Ingrid's name for Swami Chidananda.

7. AWAKENING TO THE SPIRIT

1. Matt. 3:11 (AV).
2. Mark 10:25 (AV).
3. From the Greek *apokálypsis:* "lifting of the veil, revelation."
4. Bhagavad Gita, 2:23, translated by Swami Sivananda.
5. Luke 23:34 (AV).
6. Swami Brahmananda, *The Supreme Knowledge* (Rishikesh, India: The Divine Life Society, 2000), pp. 483–487.

ABOUT THE AUTHOR

Swami Muktananda of Rishikesh was raised in Quebec, Canada, in a Catholic family. Drawn to the monastic life from an early age, he met his teacher, modern-day Indian saint Swami Chidananda, when he was only nine years old. After this meeting, the young Muktananda decided to dedicate his life to God. In 2000, after studying engineering and agroeconomics and running his own company for several years, he took vows and became a monk at the Divine Life Society, founded by Swami Sivananda in 1936. He now lives at the Sivananda Ashram in Rishikesh, northern India, at the foothills of the Himalayas, where he teaches meditation and yoga philosophy, and he has also established a retreat center in Canada. He travels extensively and holds retreats in which he shares the Hindu message of nonduality that transcends all religions.